WATCHER LANGUAGE

WATCHER LANGUAGE

Prescriptions for Writing Clear English in America

Muriel A. García

iUniverse, Inc.
New York   Bloomington

Watcher Language
Prescriptions for Writing Clear English in America

iUniverse books may be ordered through booksellers or by contacting:

iUniverse
1663 Liberty Drive
Bloomington, IN 47403
www.iuniverse.com
1-800-Authors (1-800-288-4677)

Because of the dynamic nature of the Internet, any Web addresses or links contained in this book may have changed since publication and may no longer be valid. The views expressed in this work are solely those of the author and do not necessarily reflect the views of the publisher, and the publisher hereby disclaims any responsibility for them.

ISBN: 978-1-4401-2325-2 (pbk)
ISBN: 978-1-4401-2326-9 (ebk)

Library of Congress Control Number: 2009922280

Printed in the United States of America

iUniverse rev. date: 2/17/2009

Rien n'est parfait, soupira le renard.

(Nothing is perfect, sighed the fox.)

--Antoine de Saint-Exupéry, **Le Petit Prince**

PREFACE

As a long-lived watcher of languages, and especially of American English, I know that all languages, spoken and written, are complex and that no one language is better than any other. It is a bad idea to interrupt in order to "correct" a person who is speaking because one risks not being spoken to again. If we do not get the gist of what we hear, we can ask for clarification.* It would also be rude to red-pencil a child's thank-you note or a love letter and to return it for revisions.

Writing formally—to a college admissions officer, to a prospective employer, to a newspaper editor, in anticipation of delivering a speech to an educated audience, with the intention of earning a good grade on a school assignment, or in hopes of having one's work published—is an artistic endeavor. Our written language may be elegant or simple, and it should always be clear. In the following pages I label some foggy usages as symptoms, diagnose what is wrong with them, provide remedies, then prescribe therapies. Also, I provide space for the reader to write original sentences that show that he or she can compose clear, precise, and effective prose following these prescriptions.

The source of most of the following alphabetized entries is my local newspaper, which includes articles from national and international news services. I have changed some words to spare the writers embarrassment. If anyone prefers to follow a certain manual of style, I shall not start a quarrel. Professional writers may take certain liberties that create unique impressions in their readers; my purpose is simply to help Americans to write clearly.

*The companion volume, *Listener Language*, is scheduled for 2010.

ABC'S (capital letters)

Symptom: "Frank had barely mastered his **ABC's** by the age of nine."

Diagnosis: The apostrophe in this sentence is unnecessary. It makes a possessive, not a plural.

Remedy: "Frank had barely mastered his **ABCs** by the age of nine."

Prescription: Avoid using an apostrophe when writing a plural form. "Mind your Ps and Qs." Use an apostrophe when writing a possessive form. "When you buy any HP product, you get more than great technology; you get HP's outstanding service and support."

ABOUT WHOM (preposition, object pronoun)

Symptom: "There is considerable speculation **about whom might finance** the signature drive."

Diagnosis: The writer thinks that the preposition "about" requires "whom." Here, the object of the preposition "about" is the rest of the sentence.

Remedy: "There is considerable speculation **about who might finance** the signature drive."

Prescription: Use "who" as the subject of a verb in a prepositional phrase. "Richard and his brother argued over who would play first." "There is much speculation about who has the best chance of winning the election."

ACCURATE (adjective)

Symptom: "The doctor's scale was **more** accurate than his own."

Diagnosis: "Accurate" means "careful and exact; precise; adhering closely to a standard." A thing is accurate or not.

Remedy: "The doctor's scale was accurate; his own was not."

Prescription: Avoid using a comparative, such as "less" or "more," with "accurate." "The new scale is more nearly accurate than the older models." or "The new scale is accurate to within three ounces in one hundred pounds."

ADJECTIVES THAT (noun, relative pronoun)

Symptom: "The list of **adjectives that describes** the teen years is long."

Diagnosis: The list does not describe the teen years; the adjectives do.

Remedy: "The list of **adjectives that describe** the teen years is long."

Prescription: Use a plural verb after "adjectives that." "Avoid using adjectives that do not agree in number with the nouns they modify."

AGGRAVATE (verb)

Symptom: "The topic of illegal immigration often **aggravated** the television commentator."
Diagnosis: The verb "aggravate" is used in error to mean "rile" or "annoy."
Remedy: "The topic of illegal immigration often **irritated** the television commentator."
Prescription: "Aggravate" means "worsen, make more severe." "Constant scratching aggravated the inflammation in his right leg." If you are unsure of the meaning of a word, look it up in the dictionary.

ALL BUT ONE . . . WAS (phrase . . . verb)

Symptom: "**All but one** of the charges **was** dropped after a judge found significant problems with the government's case."
Diagnosis: The subject of this sentence is "all," not "one."
Remedy: "**All but one** of the charges **were** dropped after a judge found significant problems with the government's case."
Prescription: Use a plural verb to agree with a plural subject.

ALOT OF / A LOT OF (quantitative adjective phrase)

Symptom: "Although he did not have much money, John had **alot of** friends."

Diagnosis: Here, two words have been combined into one.

Remedy: "Although he did not have much money, John had **a lot of** friends." or, preferably, "Although he did not have much money, John had **many** friends."

Prescription: Like "a couple," "a few," "a dozen," "a hundred," and "a number," "a lot" contains two words. Put a space between "a" and "lot." "She has a lot of purses." Or be specific. "She has three hundred twenty-five purses." "That hen laid a dozen eggs in eleven days."

AMONGST (preposition)

Symptom: "The sheriff's deputies found the murder weapon **amongst** the flowers."

Diagnosis: The preposition "amongst" is dated and stiff.

Remedy: "The sheriff's deputies found the murder weapon **among** the flowers."

Prescription: Avoid using "amongst" in formal writing in the United States. Use "among" instead. "The archaeologist discovered several unbroken pots among the rubble."

ANYBODY'S (possessive adjective)

Symptom: "We'll beat **anybody's** price or your mattress is free!"

Diagnosis: "Anybody's price" includes the price of this advertiser.

Remedy: "We'll beat **anybody else's** price or your mattress is free!"

Prescription: Avoid beating your own price. Use "anyone" instead of "anybody" in formal writing.

AS BEST (superlative adverbial phrase)

Symptom: "The governor did **as best** he could to balance the state budget."

Diagnosis: Here, a superlative adverb is confused with a comparative.

Remedy: "The governor did **as well as** he could to balance the state budget." or "The governor did **the best** he could to balance the state budget."

Prescription: Avoid using "as" before a superlative. Use "the" instead. "Do the best you know how." Or use "as well as." "He sang as well as he used to despite having had throat surgery."

AS BEST AS (superlative adverbial phrase)

Symptom: "Mark lived **as best as** he could with little money."

Diagnosis: Here, a superlative is used erroneously in a comparative phrase.

Remedy: "Mark lived **as well as** he could with little money."

Prescription: Avoid using the superlative of an adverb in the comparative phrase "as . . . as." "Even emergencies must be explained as well as possible."

AS FAR AS (conjunctive phrase))

Symptom: "Each child is flexible **as far as** singing harmony."

Diagnosis: This sentence contains an incomplete subordinate clause.

Remedy: "Each child is flexible **as far as** singing harmony **is concerned**."

Prescription: "As far as" indicates "to the extent or to

the degree that." Add a verb to complete the subordinate clause. "As far as runners go, he is the slowest." "As far as good health is concerned, daily exercise is necessary." Or simplify. "He is the slowest runner." "Exercise is necessary for good health."

AS FAR AS / REGARDING   (conjunctive phrase / preposition)

Symptom: "**As far as** a verdict, the jury has many options."

Diagnosis: The sentence contains an incomplete construction, "as far as."

Remedy: "**Regarding** a verdict, the jury has many options." or "The jury has many options **for** a verdict."

Prescription: Avoid using "as far as" with only a noun. Substitute "about," "regarding," or "in regard to." "As the officers escorted him to the van, Mr. X had no comment regarding his plans for the future."

AS GOOD (comparative adjective)

Symptom: "Honeybees are **as good** or better than dogs at finding land mines."

Diagnosis: Here, the equal comparison "as good" is incomplete.

Remedy: "Honeybees are **as good as** or better than dogs at finding land mines."

Prescription: When comparing equals, wrap the adjective with "as . . . as." "The sequel is as bad as or even worse than the original movie."

ASSIST (verb)

Symptom: "The goal is to **assist seniors remain** in their own homes."

Diagnosis: In this sentence, "assist" is used with an infinitive that lacks "to."

Remedy: "The goal is to **assist seniors to remain** in their own homes."

Prescription: When using certain verbs with the infinitive form of another verb, write "to" before the second verb. "The principal allowed Julie to go home early on Wednesday." "The depth of the water required the crew to wear special diving suits." "He helped the prisoner to escape somehow."

AS WELL AS   (conjunctive phrase)

Symptom: "**Both** the quality of care **as well as** the cost of providing it have increased."
Diagnosis: "Both" is unnecessary in this sentence.
Remedy: "The quality of care **as well as** the cost of providing it have increased." or "**Both** the quality of care **and** the cost of providing it have increased."
Prescription: Avoid using "both" and "as well as" in the same clause. "Both good nutrition and exercise are advisable." or "Good nutrition is advisable, as well as exercise."

AWAIT FOR   (verb, preposition)

Symptom: "The students **awaited** with questions **for** the film star."
Diagnosis: It is unclear whether the students waited for the film star or had questions for the star.
Remedy: "The students with questions **waited for** the film star."
Prescription: Since "await" and "wait for" mean the same thing, use one or the other. "Thomas awaited the day when he could get his driver's license." "Joe waited for his girlfriend to finish her shift."

BADLY / BAD (adverb / adjective)

Symptom: "He felt very **badly** about the loss."
Diagnosis: In this sentence, the adverb "badly" is used in error.
Remedy: "He felt very **bad** about the loss."
Prescription: Avoid using "badly" as the opposite of "well" after the verb "feel." Use an adjective with the verb "feel." "Johnny felt bad about cheating, although he won the game." "Her sister always feels good after a shower." "Mr. Moore felt poor after he lost the money." "Now that he has had surgery, Jacob feels well."

BEGS THE QUESTION (idiom)

Symptom: "The national debt is now more than ten trillion dollars. This **begs** the question: How can higher spending continue without higher taxes?"
Diagnosis: Here, the verb "beg" is used in error.
Remedy: "The national debt is now more than ten trillion dollars. This **raises** the question: How can higher spending continue without higher taxes?"
Prescription: "Raise" or "pose" or "ask" questions. Leave the expression "begs the question" to discussions of logical fallacies and circular reasoning.

BEING RECALLED (participial phrase)

Symptom: "All three plans run the risk of **the governor being recalled** and replaced by a default Republican."

Diagnosis: "Being recalled" is the risk here, not the governor.

Remedy: "All three plans run the risk of **the governor's being recalled** and replaced by a default Republican."

Prescription: Use the possessive form of the person or thing modifying a participle or participial phrase used as a noun. "Loretta was happy about her son's receiving the Medal of Honor." "The dog's barking kept Mort awake." "We were disappointed at his having been dismissed." or "We were disappointed that he had been dismissed."

BEST / BETTER (superlative adjective / comparative adjective)

Symptom: "Which of the **two** will make the **best** leader?"

Diagnosis: The superlative form is used here to compare only two people.

Remedy: "Which of the two will make the **better** leader?"

Prescription: Use the superlative form "best" when comparing three or more people or things. "They chose the best of three hundred applicants for the job." Use "better" when comparing two people or things. "Of the two motorcycles, Harold preferred the one that got better mileage."

BEST OF ANY (superlative adjective with prepositional phrase)

Symptom: "This county had the **best** credit rating **of any** Nevada **county**."
Diagnosis: The phrase "any Nevada county" includes the one with the best credit rating. "Any" is used erroneously here.
Remedy: "This county had the **best** credit rating **of all** Nevada **counties**."
Prescription: Use the superlative ("best," "most," "highest," "fastest," etc.) when comparing more than two persons or things. "Freddie collected the most money of all seventeen volunteers." "Lancelot was the best of all the king's men." "This is the best of all possible worlds."

BETWEEN HE AND (prepositional phrase)

Symptom: "A dispute arose **between he and** his sister."
Diagnosis: The subjective form "he" is used as the object of the preposition "between."
Remedy: "A dispute arose **between him and** his sister."
Prescription: Use objective pronouns (you, me, him, her, it, us, them) with "between . . . and." "There were no secrets between him and her." "Let this remain between you and me."

BETWEEN / AMONG (preposition)

Symptom: "The idea is to seek a balance **between** pedestrians, bicycles, transit and automobiles."
Diagnosis: "Between" requires two things or two groups of things. There are four here.
Remedy: "The idea is to seek a balance **among** pedestrians, bicycles, transit, and automobiles."
Prescription: Use "among" with more than two objects, "There was honor among the four thieves." "The princess found choosing among all those diamond necklaces difficult."

BETWEEN...AND...AND (preposition...conjunction ...conjunction)

Symptom: "The boys divided their time **between** work **and** play **and** church."
Diagnosis: "Between" is used here with more than two activities.
Remedy: "The boys divided their time **among** work, play, and church."
Prescription: Use "among" with more than two things or people. "Among three choices was a new car." "They divided the money among all the children."

BETWEEN EACH (preposition, adjective)

Symptom: "Place waxed paper **between each patty** before freezing the hamburgers."
Diagnosis: "Between" requires two things. "Patty" is singular here.
Remedy: "Place waxed paper **between the patties** before freezing the hamburgers."
Prescription: "Each" means "one of two or more considered individually." Avoid using "each" with "between." "Between the two oxen was a heavy yoke decorated with bells."

BETWEEN . . . OR (preposition, conjunction)

Symptom: "Ron could not distinguish **between** this photograph **or** that one."
Diagnosis: Here, "or" is used in error with "between."
Remedy: "Ron could not distinguish **between** this photograph **and** that one." or "Ron could not distinguish **between the two** photographs."
Prescription: Avoid using "between" with "or." Use "between . . . and." "Harold found himself stuck between a rock and a hard place." "The driver became lost between her house and the airport."

BETWEEN . . . THROUGH (preposition . . . preposition)

Symptom: "The discount coupons are valid **between** Christmas **through** mid-January,"
Diagnosis: In this sentence, "through" is used in error with "between."
Remedy: "The discount coupons are valid **between** Christmas **and** mid-January,"
Prescription: Use "between . . . and" when referring to two times of year. Or omit "between" and write "from Christmas through mid-January." "Luis had been unemployed from November through February." "No trips are available to Greenland between October 10 and April 3."

BETWEEN . . . TO (preposition)

Symptom: "Between fifty **to** sixty people attended the party."

Diagnosis: Here, "to" is used in error with "between."

Remedy: "Between fifty **and** sixty people attended the party."

Prescription: Avoid using "between" with "to." Write "between a hundred and a hundred fifty" or omit "between" and write "100 **to** 4,000." Use "between . . . and" when referring to two quantities or numbers. "Pick a number between one and ten."

BOTH (conjunction)

Symptom: "These atrocities have occurred **both** in Iraq, in the rest of the Middle East, in the United States, and around the globe."

Diagnosis: Four phrases are used with "both" here. "Both" is limited to two.

Remedy: "These atrocities have occurred in Iraq, in the rest of the Middle East, in the United States, and around the globe."

Prescription: Avoid using "both" with more than two things or people. "Jolene liked both Herb and George."

BOTH . . . AS WELL AS (conjunctions)

Symptom: "The clock face symbolizes **both** impending apocalypse **as well as** a military-type countdown."

Diagnosis: "As well as" is used in error with "both" in this sentence.

Remedy: "The clock face symbolizes **both** impending apocalypse **and** a military-type countdown." or "The clock face symbolizes impending apocalypse **as well as** a military-type countdown."

Prescription: With "both," use "and." Or use "as well as" without "both." "The committee examined both the shortcomings and the successes of the department." "There is a growing interest among film directors in creating computer games themselves: those derived from their movies as well as original projects."

BOTH BY (conjunction, preposition)

Symptom: "A number of potentially logical explanations have been offered **both by the industry** and **its critics**."

Diagnosis: In this sentence, "by the industry" and "its critics" are not parallel constructions.

Remedy: "A number of potentially logical explanations have been offered **by both the industry** and **its critics**." or "A number of potentially logical explanations have been offered both **by the industry** and **by its critics**."

Prescription: Use parallel constructions after "both." The principle of parallel construction requires that expressions of similar content and function be outwardly similar. "Miss Wilson travels by both train and bus."

BOTH BY (conjunction, preposition)

Symptom: "John was moved both **by the book** and **the movie** it inspired."

Diagnosis: "By the book" and "the movie" are not parallel constructions.

Remedy: "John was moved by both **the book** and **the movie** it inspired." or "John was moved both **by the book** and **by the movie** it inspired."

Prescription: After "both," use parallel constructions. The principle of parallel construction requires that expressions of similar content and function be outwardly similar. "The alien explorers arrived both by air and by sea."

BOTH FROM (conjunction, preposition)

Symptom: "Many people suffer **both from** depression and schizophrenia."

Diagnosis: In this sentence, "both" is positioned incorrectly.

Remedy: "Many people suffer **from both** depression and schizophrenia." or "Many people suffer both **from** depression and **from** schizophrenia."

Prescription: After "both," use parallel constructions. The principle of parallel construction requires that expressions of similar content and function be outwardly similar. "The old mountain climber suffered both from exhaustion and from muscle cramps." "Michael's ancestors were from both Ireland and Italy."

BOTH . . . OR (conjunctions)

Symptom: "The decor is suitable for **both** a guest room **or** a baby's room."

Diagnosis: In this sentence, the word "or" is used in error with "both."

Remedy: "The decor is suitable for **both** a guest room **and** a baby's room." or "The decor is suitable for **either** a guest room **or** a baby's room."

Prescription: "Both" requires two things connected by "and." Use "both" with "and." Use "either" with "or."

BOTH THE ... (conjunction, definite article)

Symptom: "The response to both **the book** and **movie** was strong."

Diagnosis: "The book" and "movie" are not parallel constructions.

Remedy: "The response to both **the book** and **the movie** was strong."

Prescription: After "both," use parallel constructions. The principle of parallel construction requires that expressions of similar content and function be outwardly similar. "Both chocolate and tea contain small amounts of caffeine."

CANNOT HELP BUT (verb phrase, conjunction)

Symptom: "The audience **cannot help but** laugh."

Diagnosis: Here, "but" is used in error.

Remedy: "The audience **cannot help laughing**."

Prescription: In this sentence, the verb "help" means "refrain from," and requires a verbal noun (gerund) or a gerundive phrase as its object. Omit the word "but" after "cannot help." "Dennis the Menace could not help annoying Mr. Wilson."

CENTER AROUND (verb, preposition)

Symptom: "The discussion **centered around** crime prevention."

Diagnosis: Here, the preposition "around" is used in error with the verb "centered."

Remedy: "The discussion centered **on** crime prevention."

Prescription: The verb "centered" means "be concentrated or focused." Use "center in" or "center on." "All the recommendations center on ways to reduce noise." "His problems are centered in his past." Or use "revolve around." "This boy's world revolves around sex, or the discussion of it." Or use "focus on." "The committee's report focused on safety measures."

> *The center's in the middle.*
> *From the midst it cannot stray;*
> *And things may go around it,*
> *But not the other way.*

CHILDREN WHO (noun, relative pronoun)

Symptom: "They raised millions of dollars to aid the one in five **children who does** not have enough to eat."

Diagnosis: In this sentence, "who" refers to "children," and is plural. The verb "does" is singular, and does not agree in number with "who."

Remedy: "They raised millions of dollars to aid the one in five **children who do** not have enough to eat."

Prescription: Use a plural verb with a plural subject. "Only one in five hundred thousand adults who drive on that road has an accident."

misplaced modifier

Symptom: "**While driving to work last week, a big black dog** crossed in front of my car."

Diagnosis: This sentence has a dog driving a car.

Remedy: "**While I was driving to work last week, a big black dog** crossed in front of my car."

Prescription: Avoid hitting big black dogs that drive cars.

CHOICE BETWEEN . . . OR (noun, preposition . . . conjunction)

Symptom: "People sometimes have to make a choice **between** spending on gasoline **or** groceries."
Diagnosis: Here, "or" is used in error with "between."
Remedy: "People sometimes have to make a choice **between** spending on gasoline **and buying** groceries." or "People sometimes have to make a choice: **to spend** on gasoline, or **to buy** groceries."
Prescription: When using "between," use "and," not "or." Make sure that the constructions after these words are parallel, too. "Maria had to choose between marrying Sam and taking a world cruise with her grandmother."

CO-CONSPIRATOR (noun)

Symptom: "Brutus was a **co-conspirator** in the plot to assassinate Julius Caesar."
Diagnosis: "Co-" is redundant here.
Remedy: "Brutus was a **conspirator** in the plot to assassinate Julius Caesar."
Prescription: "Co-" means the same thing as "con," "with, together." Omit needless word forms. "All seventeen conspirators have been arrested and charged with counterfeiting."

comma placement

Symptom: "Local gamers, **video-game retailers and parents**, agree."

Diagnosis: Either video-game retailers and parents are local gamers, or a comma is misplaced in this sentence.

Remedy: "Local gamers, **video-game retailers,** and parents agree."

Prescription: Use commas to separate elements in a list. Do not use a comma between a subject and a verb. "Criminals, law-enforcement officers, and hunters use firearms for different purposes."

Comparisons

Symptom: "Research has shown that Product Y is at least **as effective**, if not more so, **as** Product X."

Diagnosis: An equal comparison is mixed with a second comparison here.

Remedy: "Research has shown that Product Y is at least **as effective as**, if not more so **than**, Product X." or "Research has shown that Product Y is at least **as effective as** Product X, if not more so."

Prescription: Wrap "as . . . as" around an adjective when making an equal comparison. "Mary Martin sang "I'm as corny as Kansas in August.'"

COMPLETE (adjective)

Symptom: "The list of members is **more** complete now."
Diagnosis: "Complete" means "full, whole, entire, not lacking any component parts." A thing is complete or not.
Remedy: "The list of members is **nearly** complete now."
Prescription: Avoid using a comparative, such as "less" or "more," with "complete." "That is a complete waste of time."

COMPROMISE / COMPRISE (verb)

Symptom: "The National Guard and military reserve units **compromise** about forty percent of the forces in Iraq."
Diagnosis: Here, forces in Iraq are placed in danger by other military forces because of the verb "compromise."
Remedy: "The National Guard and military reserve units **comprise** about forty percent of the forces in Iraq."
Prescription: "Compromise" means "expose or make liable to danger, suspicion, or disrepute." "Consorting with

prostitutes compromised the bank president's reputation."
"Comprise" means "consist of" or "constitute." "Water is
comprised of two parts hydrogen and one part oxygen."
If you are unsure of a word's meaning, look it up in the
dictionary.

COULD CARE LESS (verb phrase)

Symptom: "Many teenagers **could care less** about listening
to classical music."
Diagnosis: If one could care less, then one must care a
great deal now. This expression, "could care less," means
the opposite of what the writer intended.
Remedy: "Many teenagers **could not care less** about
listening to classical music." or "Many teenagers **care
less** about listening to classical music than they do about
listening to rap at top volume."
Prescription: Avoid using catch phrases in formal writing.
Take care!

COULD NOT HELP BUT (verb phrase, conjunction)

Symptom: "They **could not help but be** pleased that
Saddam's control of Iraq was finished."

Diagnosis: In this sentence, "but" is used in error.

Remedy: "They **could not help being** pleased that Saddam's control of Iraq was finished."

Prescription: Avoid using "but" after "could not help." Use a gerund ending in "ing." "Jack could not help crying whenever he chopped onions."

COUNTRIES THAT ... (noun, relative pronoun)

Symptom: "Is this nation going to be in the group of **countries that tortures** people, or in the group of **countries that does not**?"

Diagnosis: In this sentence, "that" refers to the plural noun "countries," but its verb, "tortures," is singular.

Remedy: "Is this nation going to be in the group of **countries that torture** people, or in the group of **countries that do not**?"

Prescription: Use a plural verb with a plural subject. "In countries that have no oil of their own, such as France and Spain, solar power for generating electricity is gaining in popularity."

COUPLE (noun)

Symptom: "The board had overturned only ten decisions in the past **couple** years."

Diagnosis: Here, "couple" is used erroneously as an adjective.

Remedy: "The board had overturned only ten decisions in the past **couple of** years." or "The board had .overturned only ten decisions in the past **few** years."

Prescription: Avoid using "couple" with a plural noun in formal writing. Use "a couple of," "a few," or "two." "In a couple of instances, Jerry admitted, he may have been wrong."

A COUPLE HUNDRED (number)

Symptom: "Over five hundred are transferring out of the school district and only **a couple hundred** are coming in from other districts."

Diagnosis: "A couple" is used in error, without "of."

Remedy: "Over five hundred are transferring out of the school district and only **about two hundred** are coming in from other districts."

Prescription: Use "of" after "a couple," or use "two." "If Morey could just get his hands on a couple of thousand dollars, he would be able to buy the used car."

CRITERIA (plural noun)

Symptom: "The **criteria** for success **is** excellent performance."

Diagnosis: This sentence contains a plural subject and a singular verb.

Remedy: "The **criterion** for success is excellent performance." or "The **criteria** for success **are** excellent performance **and** persistence."

Prescription: Use "criterion" as the singular form and "criteria" as the plural form of this noun. "The criterion, or standard on which a judgment or decision may be based, is set by the judges themselves." "Sylvia selected three criteria for the designer of her house to use: comfort, modernity, and spaciousness."

DATA (plural noun)

Symptom: "Besides raising ethical questions, the **data** also **paints** a troubling picture."

Diagnosis: The word "data" is plural and is used with a singular verb here.

Remedy: "Besides raising ethical questions, the **data** also **paint** a troubling picture."

Prescription: Use a plural verb with "data." It is the Latin word for "things given." Or use the word "information" with a singular verb. "The information we have suggests a decline in motorcycle accidents."

DATA THAT . . . (plural noun, relative pronoun)

Symptom: "She discovered a growing body of medical **data that suggests** health benefits for the poor have declined."
Diagnosis: A singular verb is used in error here. The word "data" is plural. The word "that" refers to "data."
Remedy: "She discovered a growing body of medical **data that suggest** health benefits for the poor have declined."
Prescription: Use a plural verb with a plural subject. "Not all the data have come in yet."

DESSERT / DESERT (noun)

Symptom: "He walked through the **dessert** to reach San Diego."
Diagnosis: "Dessert" is the final course of a meal, and sometimes consists of something sticky or gooey. Can you picture the man's boots?
Remedy: "He walked through the **desert** to reach San Diego."

Prescription: If you are unsure of the spelling of a word, look it up in the dictionary. Keep your feet out of food.

DIFFERENT THAN (adjective phrase)

Symptom: "Einstein's brain was **different than** other brains."

Diagnosis: The word "different" is used in error as a comparative.

Remedy: "Einstein's brain was **different from** other brains."

Prescription: The word "than" usually introduces the second element in a comparison, as in "larger than" or "smaller than." "Different" is applied to persons or things that are not alike or are separate. Use "different from." "The mental development of a seven-year-old is much different from that of a twelve-year-old." "Mammals are different from other animals." "The information age will operate with a completely different set of rules from those that currently drive Washington politics." Use "than" after comparatives, such as "smaller," "more beautiful," "heavier." "Water is heavier than air." "Goliath was much taller than David."

DISBURSE / DISPERSE (verb)

Symptom: "The police **disbursed** the crowd."
Diagnosis: The verb "disburse" is used in error here.
.Remedy: "The police **dispersed** the crowd."
Prescription: "Disburse" means "pay out, expend." "The club's treasurer disbursed the members' dues to fund the scholarship." "Disperse" means "scatter, cause to go in different directions." "The crystal chandelier dispersed the sunlight, creating rainbows on the walls." If you are unsure of a word's meaning, look it up in the dictionary.

DO'S AND DON'TS (idiom)

Symptom: "Ms. G explained some of the **do's and dont's** of sharing medical information."
Diagnosis: Here, an apostrophe is used in error to form a plural.
Remedy: "Ms. G explained some of the **dos and don'ts** of sharing medical information."
Prescription: Avoid using an apostrophe to make a plural. "There is now a great disparity between the haves and have nots." "She said her thank yous before leaving."

DRUG (past-tense verb)

Symptom: "The men **drug** the bodies down the street."
Diagnosis: Here, "drug" is an erroneous past-tense form of the verb "drag."
Remedy: "The men **dragged** the bodies down the street."
Prescription: Use the past tense form "dragged." "The tow truck dragged the car to the junk yard."

EACH (adjective)

Symptom: "**The players each** receive a trophy."
Diagnosis: "The players" is a plural noun phrase. "Each" is a singular adjective.
Remedy: "**The players all** receive trophies." or "**Each player** receives a trophy."
Prescription: Use a singular noun or pronoun and a singular verb with "each." "Each woman has donated money to her favorite charity."

EACH (pronoun)

Symptom: "**Each** of the films **star** Jim Carrey."
Diagnosis: There is disagreement between subject and verb here.
Remedy: "**Each** of the films **stars** Jim Carrey." or "**Both** films **star** Jim Carrey." or "**All** the films **star** Jim Carrey."
Prescription: Use a singular verb with the pronoun "each." "Each of the choices sounds delicious."

EITHER . . . OR (disjunctive correlatives)

Symptom: "**Either** the attorney **or** the city **were** free to terminate the contract at will."
Diagnosis: Here, the plural verb "were" is used with the singular subject "city."
Remedy: "**Either** the attorney **or** the city **was** free to terminate the contract at will."
Prescription: "Either" means "one or the other of two." The number (singular or plural) of the verb agrees with the subject after "or." "Either the chief financial officer or his secretary has that information." "Either the Sharks or the Jets regularly carve their initials on the wall."

EITHER . . . OR (disjunctive correlatives)

Symptom: "Contestants choose to **either** compete as a team **or** as individuals."
Diagnosis: This sentence lacks parallelism. "Compete" is not like "as individuals."
Remedy: "Contestants choose to compete **either** as a team **or** as individuals."
Prescription: Use the same part of speech after "either" and "or." "Either she was mistaken, or she really did see a ghost." "You may either go or stay." "They are either too young or too old." "Either the mayor or the councilman will attend the ribbon-cutting ceremony."

EMIGRATE / IMMIGRATE (verb)

Symptom: "Having legally emigrated **here**, Mr. Ybarra was able to find work on Wall Street."
Diagnosis: There is confusion about the meaning of the word "emigrate."
Remedy: "Having legally **immigrated** here, Mr. Ybarra was able to find work on Wall Street."
Prescription: "Emigrate" means "move out." "Immigrate" means "move in." Distinguish between these similar words. The prefixes change the meaning. "Mr. Hoffman emigrated from Germany at the beginning of the Twentieth Century. He and many other Germans who immigrated

to small towns in Pennsylvania were called 'Pennsylvania Dutch.'"

_____

_____

_____

_____

ENORMITY (noun)

Symptom: "We must not minimize the **enormity** of the task ahead."

Diagnosis: The noun "enormity" is used inappropriately in this sentence.

Remedy: "We must not minimize the **enormousness** of the task ahead." or "We must not minimize the **difficulty** of the task ahead."

Prescription: "Enormity" means "outrageousness" or "excessive wickedness." "The enormity of the massacre made the survivors wail." If you are unsure of a word's meaning, look it up in the dictionary.

_____

_____

_____

_____

casey cook 09

misplaced modifier

Symptom: "**Lying on the gurney, the warden** asked the condemned man if he had any last words."

Diagnosis: In this sentence, the warden is lying on the gurney. Perhaps he is commiserating with the condemned man.

Remedy: "The warden asked **the condemned man lying on the gurney** if he had any last words."

Prescription: Make sure that a modifying phrase is next to the person or thing it describes. "The professor scowled at the student copying from another's paper."

EVERY (adjective)

Symptom: "**Every** child has **their** own crayons."
Diagnosis: The plural possessive form "their" is used here with a singular noun phrase.
Remedy: "**Every** child has **his** own crayons."
Prescription: Use a singular possessive to refer to "**every**," "Every dog has its day." "Every man has his price."

EXASPERATE / EXACERBATE (verb)

Symptom: "That herbal treatment just **exasperated** the problem."
Diagnosis: The verb "exasperate" is used erroneously here.
Remedy: "That herbal treatment just **exacerbated** the problem."
Prescription: "Exasperate" means "make very angry or bitter; annoy greatly." Use "exasperate" with people. "Having to go to bed at seven every night exasperated eight-year old Jimmy." "Exacerbate" means "increase the severity, violence, or bitterness of; aggravate, worsen." Use "exacerbate" with problems and conditions. "Scratching exacerbates the discomfort caused by poison ivy." If you are unsure of a word's meaning, look it up in the dictionary.

FEEL BADLY (verb, adverb)

Symptom: "The CEO felt **badly** that so many employees had lost their pensions."

Diagnosis: The adverb "badly" is used erroneously here.

Remedy: "The CEO felt **bad** that so many employees had lost their pensions."

Prescription: The verb "feel" requires an adjective, such as "good," "bad," "sorry." Other sensory verbs, such as "taste," "smell," "sound," "look," and "seem," are also used with adjectives. "The pizza tasted wonderful." "The week-old garbage smelled terrible."

FEWER / LESS (adjective)

Symptom: "Once the fence is completed, **less** illegal immigrants will be able to enter the United States."

Diagnosis: In this sentence, "less" is used erroneously with a plural noun phrase.

Remedy: "Once the fence is completed, **fewer** illegal immigrants will be able to enter the United States."

Prescription: Use "less" with a quantity. "Less than two-thirds of a cup of flour is used in that cake recipe." Use "fewer" with a plural noun or noun phrase. "Fewer than two hundred men attended the rally."

FOR- / FORE- (prefix)

Symptom: "Overweight people will have to **forego** dessert,"

Diagnosis: There is confusion about the meanings of "for-" and "fore-."

Remedy: "Overweight people will have to **forgo** dessert."

Prescription: Distinguish between the meanings of these two prefixes. Use "for-" to indicate "away," "apart," "off," or "involving exclusion or prohibition," or to negate the attached verb. "Forbear" means "hold back, abstain, be patient." "Forbid" means "command not (to do)." "Forgo" means "go without." Use "fore-" to indicate "before." "Forebear" means "ancestor." "Forebode" means "indicate beforehand." "Forecast," "foreclose," "foregoing" and "foregone," "forelegs," "forehead," and "foremost" are other examples.

FORWORD (noun)

Symptom: "Louis Capet mentioned Marc's grandmother in the **forword** to his book."

Diagnosis: A word is misspelled in this sentence.

Remedy: "Louis Capet mentioned Marc's grandmother in the **foreword** to his book."

Prescription: "Forword" is not a real word. If you are unclear about how to spell a word, look it up in the dictionary.

FROM BETWEEN (prepositions)

Symptom: "Mr. X is among patients who died **from between** the mid-1880s **and** 1924."

Diagnosis: In this sentence, "from" is unnecessary.

Remedy: "Mr. X is among patients who died **between** the mid-1880s **and** 1924." or "Mr. X is among patients who died **from** the mid-1880s **to** 1924."

Prescription: Avoid using two prepositions together. Use either "between . . . and" or "from . . . to." "Children between the ages of three and seven love fairy tales." or "Children from three to seven love fairy tales."

FROM WHENCE (prepositional phrase)

Symptom: "They will be allowed to return to the communities **from whence** they came."

Diagnosis: The word "whence" is used erroneously here.

Remedy: "They will be allowed to return to the communities from **which** they came."
Prescription: "Whence" already means "from where." Avoid using the word "whence" altogether. It is archaic.

GENDER / SEX (noun)

Symptom: "Cecilia looked away from the ultrasound screen, wanting her baby's **gender** to be a surprise."
Diagnosis: "Gender" is used here instead of "sex," perhaps because the writer is modest; or there may be confusion because nouns and their adjectives in some languages are called "masculine," "feminine," or "neuter."
Remedy: "Cecilia looked away from the ultrasound screen, wanting her baby's **sex** to be a surprise."
Prescription: In the remedial sentence, "sex" means "the character of being male or female." "Kevin attracted members of the opposite sex." "Women are called the fair sex." Use "sex" to denote being male or female. Use "gender" when discussing nouns and pronouns. "Gender" comes from the Latin noun "*genus*," which means "birth, origin, species, race, kind." This word is applied to noun forms in some languages, such as Greek, Romance languages, and German, and to adjectives modifying them. "In German, adjectives agree in number and in gender with the nouns they modify." A related word is the French "genre," which means "kind or type, as of art, film, or literature."

A HALF AN INCH (phrase)

Symptom: "Georgina was **a half an inch** taller than her mother."

Diagnosis: There is an unnecessary indefinite article in this sentence.

Remedy: "Georgina was **half an inch** taller than her mother." or "Georgina was **a half-inch** taller than her mother."

Prescription: Avoid duplicating articles. "Harry bought half a dozen roses for his sweetheart that afternoon."

HAVE / HAS (verb)

Symptom: "Neither Dr. X nor anyone else **have** a quick solution to this problem."

Diagnosis: The plural verb "have" is used with the singular subject "anyone else."

Remedy: "Neither Dr. X nor anyone else **has** a quick solution to this problem."

Prescription: After "nor" and a singular subject, use a singular verb. "Neither the homeowners nor the new tenant has any idea how to repair the leaky pipe."

HEALTHY / HEALTHFUL (adjective)

Symptom: "Sally's mother lost twenty pounds by eating **healthy** food."

Diagnosis: Imagine how much she would have lost by eating sick food! The adjective "healthy" is used in error here.

Remedy: "Sally's mother lost twenty pounds by eating **healthful** food."

Prescription: Use "healthy" when describing a state of wellness. "Vitamins help to build healthy bodies." Use "healthful" when you mean "promoting well-being." "Healthful activities include walking, cycling, and swimming."

HE AND HIS WIFE (pronoun, conjunction, noun)

Symptom: "The presidential candidate is coming to meet **he and his wife**."

Diagnosis: The subject form "he" is used here as a direct object.

Remedy: "The presidential candidate is coming to meet **him and his wife**."

Prescription: Avoid using a subject pronoun as the object of a verb. Use an object pronoun instead. Object pronouns are "me," "you," "him," "her," "it," "us," and "them." "Four years later, the FBI agents found him and his brother in South America."

═══════════════════════════════════════

═══════════════════════════════════════

═══════════════════════════════════════

═══════════════════════════════════════

THE HIGHEST ... OF ANY (superlative adjective ... prepositional phrase)

Symptom: "Americans enjoy the **highest** standard of living **of any nation** in the world."
Diagnosis: The singular "any" is used incorrectly with "highest," a superlative.
Remedy: "Americans enjoy the **highest** standard of living **of all nations** in the world."
Prescription: Avoid using the singular "any" with a superlative. Use a superlative when comparing more than two people or things. "Restaurants have the highest failure rate of all service-sector businesses."

═══════════════════════════════════════

═══════════════════════════════════════

═══════════════════════════════════════

═══════════════════════════════════════

HOPEFULLY (adverb)

Symptom: "**Hopefully**, the fire will burn itself out by tomorrow."

Diagnosis: Fire is incapable of hope. The adverb is used erroneously here.

Remedy: "**Officials hope** the fire will burn itself out by tomorrow."

Prescription: Avoid using "hopefully" as an independent adverb. "The child looked hopefully out the window as he waited for his father to come home."

HUSBAND (noun)

Symptom: "Sally did not mind her **husband** eating in bed."

Diagnosis: "Eating in bed" is what Sally did not mind, rather than her husband.

Remedy: "Sally did not mind her **husband's** eating in bed."

Prescription: Avoid eating in bed. Always mind your spouse.

I.E. / E.G. (abbreviation)

Symptom: "Space will be needed to store materials, **i.e.,** lumber, masonry, etc. "

Diagnosis: Lumber and masonry are examples here, not

the only materials.

Remedy: "Space will be needed to store materials, **e.g.**, lumber, masonry, etc."

Prescription: Avoid using "i.e." with a partial list. This is an abbreviation of the Latin *id est*, "that is." Use "i.e." to explain or to clarify a preceding term or concept. "He was an eremite, i.e., he lived alone in the woods, miles away from his nearest neighbor." Or substitute "that is" or "namely" for "i.e." "We desire only one thing, namely, to live in peace." Use "e.g." before an example or a list of examples. This is an abbreviation of the Latin *exempli gratia*, "for the sake of example." "Some people, e.g., Eskimos, have many words for 'snow.'" "These are matters of international importance, e.g., business, politics, etc." Or substitute "such as" or "for example" for "e.g." "You can check with organizations that specialize in specific breeds, such as Dobermans."

IN CLOSE PROXIMITY TO (phrase)

Symptom: "Harry lived **in close proximity to** his mother-in law until she died of multiple stab wounds."

Diagnosis: In this sentence, the adjective "close" is redundant with "proximity."

Remedy: "Harry lived **near** his mother-in law until she died of multiple stab wounds."

Prescription: "Proximity" already means "closeness." Avoid using "close" with this noun. "There is a high school close to the power lines." "The hotel is ideally located near the beach." "The hospital's proximity to doctors' offices gives patients an advantage." Avoid utilizing gargantuan, polysyllabic language units wherever one short word will do.

═══════════════════════════════════════

═══════════════════════════════════════

═══════════════════════════════════════

═══════════════════════════════════════

incomplete construction

Symptom: "This one is **as good** or better **than** that one."
Diagnosis: "As good" is an incomplete construction.
Remedy: "This one is **as good as** or better than that one."
Prescription: When comparing equals, use "as . . . as" around the adjective. "Cecilia is as beautiful as a clear day." "That meat tasted as bad as mutton without curry."

═══════════════════════════════════════

═══════════════════════════════════════

═══════════════════════════════════════

═══════════════════════════════════════

IN TERMS OF (prepositional phrase, preposition)

Symptom: "The self-propelled rail car compares to the most modern trains in Europe **in terms of comfort**."
Diagnosis: Let me just say that in my opinion, I believe that this sentence contains far too many words that the writer does not really and truly need in order to get his or her message across to the reader.
Remedy: "The self-propelled rail car compares **in comfort**

to the most modern trains in Europe."
Prescription: Avoid needless words. Simplify. "Carl had the record in points scored that season."

IN THE 1850'S (prepositional phrase)

Symptom: "**In the 1850's**, John's great-grandfather crossed the prairies in a covered wagon."
Diagnosis: An apostrophe is used in error here to form a plural.
Remedy: "**In the 1850s**, John's great-grandfather crossed the prairies in a covered wagon."
Prescription: Avoid using an apostrophe to form a plural. "Some oldies but goodies from the 1970s can be heard on this radio station."

IRREGARDLESS OF (adjective, preposition)

Symptom: "**Irregardless of** the risks, Hank invested his life savings in one stock."
Diagnosis: The prefix **ir-** (**in-**, "not," assimilated to the **r** beginning **regardless**) creates a double negative.
Remedy: "**Regardless of** the risks, Hank invested his life savings in one stock."

Prescription: "Regardless of" means "unmindful of," "not considering." Avoid using "irregardless" in formal writing, regardless of the temptation to do so.

IT'S / ITS (pronoun and verb / possessive adjective)

Symptom: "The city is known for **it's** oak trees."
Diagnosis: No apostrophe is needed here.
Remedy: "The city is known for **its** oak trees."
Prescription: Substitute "it is" or "it has." for "it's" in formal writing. "It is a good thing." "It has been seven years." Use "its" to indicate "belonging to it" or "of it." "The dog wagged its tail." "Each machine has its own power system."

KIND / KINDS (noun)

Symptom: "**Those kind of pizzas** get all but one slice of the $30 billion racked up in total pizza sales every year."
Diagnosis: Here, a singular noun is used in error after "those."
Remedy: "**Those kinds of pizzas** get all but one slice of the $30 billion racked up in total pizza sales every year." or "**That kind of pizza gets** all but one slice of the $30

billion racked up in total pizza sales every year."

Prescription: Use "kind" after a singular and "kinds" after a plural demonstrative adjective. "No one wants to do this kind of job." or "No one wants to do these kinds of jobs."

LAID / LAY (past-tense verb)

Symptom: "Bands of guerrillas **laid** in wait at two banks yesterday."

Diagnosis: The past tense of "lay" has been used instead of the past tense of "lie" in this sentence.

Remedy: "Bands of guerrillas **lay** in wait at two banks yesterday."

Prescription: Use a direct object after "laid." "Penelope laid the book on the table." Use "lay" as the past tense of "lie." "The girls lay out in the sun yesterday."

LAY LOW (idiom)

Symptom: "After **laying low** for several weeks to grow a beard and mustache, the outlaw went back to the saloon."

Diagnosis: The present participle of the verb "lay" has been used in error instead of the present participle of "lie."

Remedy: "After **lying low** for several weeks to grow a

beard and mustache, the outlaw went back to the saloon."
Prescription: Use the verb "lie" (past tense forms "lay," "lain") with "low," "down," and other adverbs. The lion lay low in the grass before he pounced on the antelope." Use the verb "lay" (past tense forms "laid," "laid") with a direct object noun or pronoun. "The soldiers laid their weapons down."

LEAST / FEWEST (superlative adjective)

Symptom: "Those who have the **least** resources buy the most lottery tickets."
Diagnosis: There is disagreement between the adjective "least" and the noun "resources" here.
Remedy: "Those who have the **fewest** resources buy the most lottery tickets."
Prescription: Use "least" before a singular or collective noun and "fewest" before a plural noun. "The least tar," "the least number," "the least money," "the fewest children," "the fewest rainy days," "the fewest dollars."

LESS / FEWER (comparative adjective)

Symptom: "**Less** people are leaving the county."

Diagnosis: There is disagreement between the adjective "less" and the noun "people" here.

Remedy: "**Fewer people** are leaving the county."

Prescription: Use "less" before a collective noun or a quantity. Use "fewer" before a plural noun when items are individuals: "less money, fewer dollars," "less hair, fewer mustaches," "fewer calories, less fat," "less than (the amount of) ten dollars," "ten (separate) items or fewer."

LIE / LAY (verb)

Symptom: "The dog responded to commands to sit, **lay** down, heel, and stay."

Diagnosis: There is confusion between the verbs "lie" (past forms "lay, lain") and "lay" (past forms "laid, laid").

Remedy: "The dog responded to commands to sit, **lie** down, heel, and stay."

Prescription: Use "lie" alone, without an object. "Dad likes to lie on the sofa after work." "As he lay dying, his son wept." "The book had lain on that table for a whole month." Use "lay" with an object. "Lay the book on the table." "They laid the corpse out for viewing." "The hen had laid no eggs for a week." "Now I lay me down to sleep." "A duck can lay eggs, but she cannot lay down. Down must be plucked off."

LIKE / AS IF (preposition / conjunction)

Symptom: "It seemed **like** it should still be summer vacation."
Diagnosis: Here, a clause follows the preposition "like."
Remedy: "It seemed **as if** it should still be summer vacation." or "It still seemed **like** summer vacation."
Prescription: Use "like" before a noun or pronoun. Use "as if" before a clause. "His face turned pale, as if he had seen a ghost." "His face turned pale, like that of a ghost." "It looked like rain." or "It looked as if it would rain."

LOAN / LEND (noun / verb)

Symptom: "He asked the city council to **loan** the agency $40,000."
Diagnosis: The noun "loan" is used as a verb here.
Remedy: "He asked the city council to **lend** the agency $40,000."
Prescription: Use "loan" as a noun and "lend" as a verb. "The bank manager approved a $50,000 loan." "Joe lent fifty dollars to his brother-in-law last week." "Lend us a loan of your noserag." (James Joyce)

THE LOWEST OF ANY   (superlative adjective, prepositional phrase)

Symptom: "California has **the lowest** credit rating **of any** state **government** in America."

Diagnosis: Here, a superlative is used with "any," a singular form.

Remedy: "California has **the lowest** credit rating **of all** state **governments** in America."

Prescription: Avoid using a superlative adjective with "any." A superlative is used to compare more than two things or people. Use a plural noun or pronoun with a superlative. "Carl received the lowest of three hundred scores."

A MAN LIKE (phrase)

Symptom: "You are very lucky to have **a man like** Mr. X representing you."

Diagnosis: Who represents you? Mr. X, or a man like him?

Remedy: "You are very lucky to have **Mr. X** representing you."

Prescription: Avoid using "a man like," "a woman like," "a person like," or "someone like." Use the actual person instead. "We enjoy hearing Andrea Bocelli sing Neapolitan songs."

___

MEDIA (plural noun)

Symptom: "The **media is** partly responsible for violence."

Diagnosis: The subject is plural and the verb is singular here.

Remedy: "The **media are** partly responsible for violence."

Prescription: Avoid using a singular verb with a plural subject. Use a plural verb with "media." The media include newspapers, magazines, books, pamphlets, television, the movies, the Internet, and advertising. A single one of these is a "medium." "Through the medium of television, Juan learned to speak English quite well."

___

misplaced modifier

Symptom: "**At the age of six, Ricky's father** died."

Diagnosis: It is probably impossible to become a father when one is so young.

Remedy: "**When Ricky was six**, his father died."

Prescription: Place a modifying phrase next to the person

it modifies, or rewrite the sentence. "Paddling the kayak, the Eskimo spotted a wounded elk." Or "As he paddled the kayak, the Eskimo spotted a wounded elk."

---

misplaced modifier

Symptom: "**As a valued traveler, I** want to stay up to date with your interests."
Diagnosis: Who is the valued traveler here? The writer?
Remedy: "**Because you are a valued traveler, I** want to stay up to date with your interests."
Prescription: Avoid putting a modifying phrase in an awkward position. "As a veteran, Joe had access to free hospital services."

---

misplaced modifier

Symptom: "His weak eyes kept him from **the sky, a condition** now easily treated."
Diagnosis: In this sentence, "a condition" apparently refers to "the sky."
Remedy: "His weak eyes kept him from **the sky**. Nearsightedness is a condition now easily treated."
Prescription: Avoid putting a modifying phrase in an

awkward position. "Shuffling along the boardwalk, Shelly avoided other people when they came too close."

MOMENTARILY (adverb)

Symptom: "The plane will be landing **momentarily**."
Diagnosis: The adverb "momentarily" is used in error here. Do not unfasten your seat belt yet, because the plane will be taking off again right away.
Remedy: "The plane will be landing **in a moment**."
Prescription: Use "momentarily" when you mean "for a moment." "Susan's eyes lost their focus momentarily."

MORE ACCURATELY (comparative adverb)

Symptom: "They replaced the outdated formula with one that **more accurately** reflects current interest rates."
Diagnosis: A formula is accurate, inaccurate, or nearly accurate.
Remedy: "They replaced the outdated formula with one that **accurately** reflects current interest rates."
Prescription: Avoid using a comparative or superlative with "accurately." "The new computer accurately transfers data from the old one."

MORE COMPLETE (comparative adjective)

Symptom: "The list of members is **more** complete now."
Diagnosis: A thing is complete or not.
Remedy: "The list of members is **nearly** complete now."
Prescription: "Complete" means "full, whole, entire, not lacking any component parts." Avoid using a comparative, such as "less" or "more," with "complete." "Only strangers are complete, total, and perfect."

MORE PRECISE (comparative adjective)

Symptom: "A **more precise** number can be derived."
Diagnosis: A number is precise or not.
Remedy: "A **precise** number can be derived."
Prescription: "Precise" already means "minutely exact, strictly defined, accurately stated." Avoid using a comparative, such as "less" or "more," with "precise." "Thanks to new technology, the precise amount of blood sugar can be measured."

MORE...THAN ANY (comparative adjective or adverb, singular adjective)

Symptom: "Bill Gates has more money than **any** American."

Diagnosis: Here "any" means "one, no matter which, of more than two." Bill Gates is American, is he not? Does he have more money than he has?

Remedy: "Bill Gates has more money than **any other** American."

Prescription: Use "other" after an unequal comparison with "any." "Midas was richer than any other man." "The Sears Tower is taller than any other building in Chicago." "The rocket carrying the Mars Rover went farther than any other space ship had gone." "Mrs. X is more responsible than any other candidate."

misplaced modifier

Symptom: "**At its deepest point, an iron ball** would take more than an hour to sink to the ocean floor."

Diagnosis: Here, the "deepest point" is in the iron ball.

Remedy: "An iron ball would take more than an hour to sink to **the ocean floor at its deepest point**."

Prescription: Place a modifying phrase next to the thing it describes. "The heavy drapes kept out the sunlight shining on the windows."

=========

=========

=========

=========

MOST (superlative adjective)

Symptom: "Mr. X received the **most** votes of **any** Republican candidate."
Diagnosis: This example contains a superlative, but compares votes of only two people, namely, Mr. X and a Republican candidate.
Remedy: "Mr. X received the **most** votes of **all** Republican **candidates**."
Prescription: A superlative compares more than two people or things. Use "of all" after a superlative. "Jennie was the most accomplished speller of all the girls in the ninth grade."

=========

=========

=========

=========

MOST ANY (superlative adjective, singular adjective)

Symptom: "**Most any** afternoon the wind would come up."
Diagnosis: The superlative "most" is used in error with a singular adjective here.
Remedy: "**Almost any** afternoon the wind would come

up." or "**Most afternoons** the wind would come up."
Prescription: Avoid using "most" with the singular adjective "any." Use "almost" or "nearly" instead. "In almost any other city, a skyscraper would stand out."

MOST ANYONE   (superlative adjective, singular pronoun)

Symptom: "**Most anyone** can get a job."
Diagnosis: The superlative form "most" is used in error with the singular pronoun "anyone."
Remedy: "**Almost anyone** can get a job." or "**Nearly everyone** can get a job." or "**Most people** can get jobs."
Prescription: Avoid using "most" with the singular pronoun "anyone." Use "almost" or "nearly" instead. "These nightshirts will fit almost anyone." "Nearly anyone who wants to can wear black." Or use "most" with a plural noun. "Most dieters fail to keep the weight off."

MOST EVERY (superlative adjective, singular adjective)

Symptom: "In summer, Sarah gazed at the stars **most** every evening."
Diagnosis: The superlative "most" is used in error with a

singular pronoun here.

Remedy: "In summer, Sarah gazed at the stars al**most** every evening."

Prescription: Avoid writing "every" after "most." Use "almost every" or "nearly every," or use "most" with a plural noun. "Almost every time he threw the ball, he missed the basket." "Most dogs eat meat." "This new law is important to nearly every citizen."

MOST EVERYONE (superlative adjective, singular pronoun)

Symptom: "**Most everyone** has heard the last movement of Beethoven's Ninth Symphony."

Diagnosis: The superlative "most" is used in error with a singular pronoun here.

Remedy: "**Almost everyone** has heard the last movement of Beethoven's Ninth Symphony."

Prescription: Avoid using "most" with a singular pronoun. Use "almost" or "nearly" instead. "Nearly everyone likes chocolate." Or use a plural noun after "most." "Most people can walk upright."

MOST EVERYTHING (superlative adjective, singular pronoun)

Symptom: "**Most everything** else requires effort, even if I enjoy that effort."
Diagnosis: The superlative "most" is used in error with a singular pronoun here.
Remedy: "**Almost everything** else requires effort, even if I enjoy that effort."
Prescription: Avoid using "most" with a singular noun or pronoun. Substitute "almost." "Gene liked almost everything on the menu."

MOST . . . OF ANY (superlative adjective, prepositional phrase)

Symptom: "California has the **most voters of any state**."
Diagnosis: California is also a state. Does it have more voters than itself?
Remedy: "California has the **most voters of all the states**."
Prescription: Avoid using "most" with "of any." Substitute "of all." "The conservative received the most votes of **all** Republican candidates on the state ballot." "Of all the boys, Jamie had the most freckles."

MOST UNIQUE (superlative adjective)

Symptom: "The wallpaper had a **most unique** flower pattern."

Diagnosis: Here, the adverb "most" is used in error with the adjective "unique."

Remedy: "The wallpaper had a **unique** flower pattern."

Prescription: The word "unique" means "without equal, matchless." Avoid using a comparative or superlative with this "incomparable" adjective, just as you would with the adjective "alone." "Kurt believed that each snowflake was unique."

NEED (verb)

Symptom: "That disparity does not **need be** resolved right now."

Diagnosis: The verb "need" needs to have an infinitive after it here.

Remedy: "That disparity does not **need to be** resolved right now."

Prescription: Use an infinitive after the verb "need." "Florence needs to have her head examined." "Aaron needed to go into the city."

NEITHER (pronoun)

Symptom: "Neither of those answers **were** right."
Diagnosis: A singular subject is used here with a plural verb.
Remedy: "Neither of those answers **was** right."
Prescription: "Neither" means "not either one of the two." Use a singular verb after "neither." "Neither boy wears a coat." "Neither of the two has been invited." "Neither of the two women wants to go."

NEITHER . . . NOR (disjunctive correlatives)

Symptom: "The agencies are **neither required** to check permits **nor to** verify deals with landowners."
Diagnosis: This sentence lacks parallel constructions after "neither" and "nor."
Remedy: "The agencies are required **neither to check** permits **nor to verify** deals with landowners."
Prescription: Use words that are the same part of speech after "neither" and "nor." "Neither by selling his stereo nor by begging for alms could he raise the money he needed." "Neither for love nor for money will he tell a lie."

NEW INNOVATIONS (adjective, noun)

Symptom: "Under his leadership, several **new innovations** were introduced and realized."

Diagnosis: The adjective "new" is redundant here.

Remedy: "Under his leadership, several **innovations** were introduced and realized."

Prescription: "Innovation" already means "a new method, custom, device, or way of doing things." Avoid using redundant adjectives such as "new" or "novel" with "innovation." "Another innovation was the atomic clock."

NOT ONLY (correlative conjunction)

Symptom: The park will **not only include** an Olympic-size pool, but soccer fields, a bicycle path, and hiking trails."

Diagnosis: The correlative conjunction "not only" is misplaced here.

Remedy: "The park will **include not only** an Olympic-size pool, but **also** soccer fields, a bicycle path, and hiking trails."

Prescription: Use words that are the same part of speech after "not only" and "but also." "Not only does he violate the law, but also he scoffs at all rules." "The robber ordered him to turn over not only his money, but also a Pepsi."

NOT ONLY . . . AND NOT ONLY (conjunctions)

Symptom: "Ruthless enemies seek to destroy **not only** our nation **and not only** to destroy all free nations **but** to destroy freedom as a way of life."
Diagnosis: The writer has used "not only" unnecessarily twice and "to destroy" three times in this sentence.
Remedy: "Ruthless enemies seek to destroy **not only** our nation **but** all free nations and freedom as a way of life."
Prescription: Avoid needless repetition.

NOT ONLY . . . BUT ALSO (correlative conjunctions)

Symptom: "It damaged **not only our legal system, but also poisoned** our political process."
Diagnosis: This sentence lacks parallelism.
Remedy: "It **not only damaged** our legal system, **but also poisoned** our political process."
Prescription: Use words that are the same part of speech after "not only" and "but also." "He drank not only on weekends but also during the week." "John likes not only to draw, but also to paint."

A NUMBER OF (noun phrase, preposition)

Symptom: "A number of patients **has** died of influenza."
Diagnosis: There is disagreement between subject and verb here.
Remedy: "A number of patients **have** died of influenza."
Prescription: "A number of" is specific and plural. Use a plural verb with "a number of." Test by substituting "a few," "a couple of," "a hundred," or "several" for "a number of." "A number of students never receive a high-school diploma."

THE NUMBER OF (noun phrase, preposition)

Symptom: "The number of elderly **have** increased dramatically."
Diagnosis: Here, the verb disagrees with the subject.
Remedy: "The number of elderly **has** increased dramatically."
Prescription: "The number" is nonspecific and singular. Use a singular verb with "the number of." "The total number of stars is unknown."

OFF OF (prepositions)

Symptom: "The police discovered the man's body in a field **off of** Highway 96."
Diagnosis: The word "of" is unnecessary in this sentence.
Remedy: "The police discovered the man's body in a field **off** Highway 96."
Prescription: Use the preposition "off" alone, without "of." "Mother told Joe to get his feet off the table." "Keep off the grass." "Finally, Vance was off the hook." "The president took some of the heat off his attorney general."

ONE IN FOUR (pronoun, prepositional phrase)

Symptom: "**One in four** nursing homes nationwide **have** violations that put patients at risk."
Diagnosis: Here, the verb disagrees with the subject.
Remedy: "**One in four** nursing homes nationwide **has** violations that put patients at risk."
Prescription: Use a singular verb with a singular subject. "One in four thousand cattle on that ranch weighs more than a ton."

ONE OF JUST FIVE . . . THAT (pronoun, prepositional phrase, relative pronoun)

Symptom: "California is one of **just five states that does** not post this information on the Internet."

Diagnosis: California is not the only one, is it? "That" refers to "states," and is used in error with a singular verb.

Remedy: "California is one of just five **states that do** not post this information on the Internet."

Prescription: When "that" is the subject of the verb in a dependent clause, and when "that" refers to more than one, use a plural verb in the dependent clause. "One of only three companies that offer rebates has gone bankrupt." Recognize that three companies offer rebates, and one has gone bankrupt. Is that clear now?

ONE OF THE FACTORS THAT . . . (pronoun, prepositional phrase, relative pronoun)

Symptom: "Doctor-shopping is one of the **factors that has** driven up costs in California."

Diagnosis: That" refers to "factors," and so "that" is also plural. However, the verb "has" is singular.

Remedy: "Doctor-shopping is one of the **factors that have** driven up costs in California."

Prescription: When "that" is the subject of the verb in a dependent clause, and when "that" refers to more than one, use a plural verb in the dependent clause. "One of the factors that have contributed to Hal's success is his generosity."

ONE OF THE FEW THAT (pronoun, prepositional phrase, relative pronoun)

Symptom: "Pistachio is one **of the few flavors that appeals** to me."
Diagnosis: "That" refers to "flavors," so "that" is plural, but the verb is singular here.
Remedy: "Pistachio is one **of the few flavors that appeal** to me."
Prescription: In a clause beginning with a relative pronoun subject, make the verb agree with the pronoun in number. "One of the very few things that cause him to lose his temper is standing in line for twenty minutes."

ONE OF THE THINGS THAT (pronoun, prepositional phrase, relative pronoun)

Symptom: "Lying is one of the **things that bothers** him,"
Diagnosis This sentence lacks agreement between the subject "that" and its verb in the subordinate clause.

Remedy: "Lying is one of the **things that bother** him,"
Prescription: Avoid using a singular verb after "things that." Use a plural verb. "The things that bother him **are** lying, cheating, and stealing." "Luke feared one of those things that go bump in the night." "Repaving is one of several steps that have to be taken." Or substitute "among" for "one of." "Gardening is among those things that delight her."

ONE OF THE TWO . . . THAT (pronoun, prepositional phrase, relative pronoun)

Symptom: "One of the **two missiles that is** being analyzed has a range exceeding 150 kilometers."
Diagnosis: "That" refers to "two missiles," but here, "that" is used with a singular verb.
Remedy: "One of the **two missiles that are** being analyzed has a range exceeding 150 kilometers."
Prescription: When "that" is the subject of the verb in a dependent clause, and when "that" refers to more than one, use a plural verb. "Spaghetti is one of the two Italian dishes that appeal to Jane." Jane is finicky; she likes only two kinds of pasta. One kind is spaghetti. Is that clear now?

ONE OF THOSE . . . WHO (pronoun, prepositional phrase, relative pronoun)

Symptom: "Jack was like one of **those** inexperienced mountain climbers **who thinks** all **he has** to do is make it to the next ridge."
Diagnosis: Jack is not the only person who thinks this. Many other inexperienced mountain climbers do, too.
Remedy: "Jack was like one of **those** inexperienced mountain climbers **who think** all **they have** to do is make it to the next ridge."
Prescription: When "who" is the subject of a verb, and when "who" refers to "those," use a plural verb. "Martin was one of those men who marry in haste and repent at leisure."

ONE OF THOSE PEOPLE WHO (pronoun, prepositional phrase, relative pronoun)

Symptom: "Mr. X is one of those **people who** also **complains** about airport noise."
Diagnosis: This example lacks agreement of the subject pronoun "who" and its verb in the subordinate clause. "Who" refers to "people," but the verb is singular.
Remedy: "Mr. X is one of those **people who** also **complain** about airport noise."
Prescription: Avoid using a singular verb after "people who." Use a plural verb. "People who live in glass houses

are careful writers." "He is one of those people who live in the inner city." Or substitute "among" for "one of. " "She is among those people who adore gardening." Or substitute "a person who" with a singular verb. "Mr. X is a person who hates to be late." Watch for similar constructions, such as "one of a few Mexican singers who also write novels," "one of the many readers who donate their books to the Friends of the Library."

ONLY (adjective or adverb)

Symptom: "Floyd **only** had a sixth-grade education."
Diagnosis: The word "only" is out of place. It is unclear whether Floyd was the only person with a sixth-grade education or whether he had gone only as far as the sixth grade.
Remedy: "Floyd had **only** a sixth-grade education."
Prescription: Place the word "only" in front of the word or words it limits. "Only the brave die young." "The baby cried only when she was hungry." "Mr. X. said only that he had had a long day." "Pull this handle only in case of fire." "Maria desired only to become a citizen."

PARAMETERS / PERIMETERS (plural noun)

Symptom: "He offered some **parameters** to work **within**."

Diagnosis: There is confusion between "parameters" and "perimeters" here.

Remedy: "He offered **a framework within** which to work,"

Prescription: Avoid using "parameters" after the words "within the" if you mean "boundaries" or "limits." The word "parameter" means "a measure alongside." "Parameters" are best used by mathematicians dealing with constants and variables. The word "perimeter" means "a measure around." Use "within the boundaries," within the framework," "within the bounds," "within the limits," or "within the scope." "Calculus is not within the scope of my knowledge." "The commissioners started a project to develop broad limits for the county's greenbelts."

---

participle used as a noun

Symptom: "He called the chances of **the Supreme Court** ever **hearing** the case remote."

Diagnosis: The object of the preposition "of" is "hearing the case," not "the Supreme Court."

Remedy: "He called the chances of **the Supreme Court's** ever **hearing** the case remote." or "He considered it only a remote possibility that the Supreme Court would ever hear the case."

Prescription: Use the possessive form of a noun or pronoun before a participial phrase used as the object of a preposition. "Derek's parole depended on his obeying all the laws." Or rewrite: "Derek's parole depended on his obedience to all the laws." "The chase ended with the suspect's being shot." or "The chase ended with the shooting of the suspect."

PAY FOR (verb phrase)

Symptom: "The motorist must **pay for** towing, car storage and **a fee to retrieve** the car."

Diagnosis: One pays a fee; one does not pay for a fee.

Remedy: "The motorist must **pay for** towing, storing, and retrieving the car."

Prescription: Use "pay for" before something bought. "Lottie paid seventy thousand dollars for her new car."

misplaced modifier

Symptom: "Margie gazed at the **flowers growing from her window**."

Diagnosis: In this sentence, the flowers are growing from the window.

Remedy: "**From her window, Margie** gazed at the flowers growing."

Prescription: Place a modifying phrase next to the word it describes. "Standing at the top of the mountain, Luis could keep an eye on the sheep."

PLEASE R.S.V.P. (interjection, abbreviation)

Symptom: "Please R.S.V.P. no later than April 22."
Diagnosis: In this sentence, "please" is redundant.
Remedy: "R.S.V.P. no later than April 22."
Prescription: "R.S.V.P." stands for "Répondez, s'il vous plaît" and means "Answer, please." Avoid using needless words.

PREDOMINATELY / PREDOMINANTLY (adverb)

Symptom: "That is the explosive **predominately** used by Middle-Eastern suicide bombers."
Diagnosis: The writer has added "-ly" incorrectly to a verb form.
Remedy: "That is the explosive **predominantly** used by Middle-Eastern suicide bombers."
Prescription: Adverbs are frequently made by adding "-ly" to adjectives. The word "predominate" is a verb. Avoid adding "-ly" to verbs. "The Stanford-Binet I.Q. test was

predominantly verbal."

PRINCIPAL / PRINCIPLE (noun)

Symptom: "The President and the Speaker of the House agreed in **principal** on an economic stimulus package."
Diagnosis: The word "principal" is used in error here.
Remedy: "The President and the Speaker of the House agreed in **principle** on an economic stimulus package."
Prescription: The noun "principal" means "head of a school" or "original amount of a debt, on which interest is calculated." "Joan paid four per cent of the principal each year." The noun "principle" means "rule, theory, notion, tenet, dogma, assumption, law." "Jeremy believed in the principle of the equality of human beings." Distinguish between these two nouns.

PROXIMITY (noun)

Symptom: "The cabin is **located in close proximity to** the lake."
Diagnosis: This sentence contains too many words.
Remedy: "The cabin is **near** the lake."
Prescription: Avoid using redundant words. Simplify. The

noun "proximity" already means "closeness." The verb form "located" is unnecessary. "The grocery store was near her house, so she walked there."

———————————————————————————
———————————————————————————
———————————————————————————
———————————————————————————

QUALITY (adjective)

Symptom: "Those are all **quality** people who have achieved great success."

Diagnosis: The word "quality" alone does not adequately describe those people.

Remedy: "Those are all **fine** people who have achieved great success."

Prescription: When used as an adjective, "quality" must itself be qualified with a word such as "high," "good," "low," "inferior," or "poor." Place a hyphen between the descriptive adjective and "quality." "The district is moving forward to ensure a high-quality education for every student." "If chefs use cheap, poor-quality ingredients, the results may not be very tasty." "She and her children stayed at a run-down Quality Inn three miles from the railway station."

———————————————————————————
———————————————————————————
———————————————————————————
———————————————————————————

THE REASON . . . IS BECAUSE . . . (subject, linking verb, adverbial clause)

Symptom: "**The reason** for his absence yesterday **is because** he was sick."

Diagnosis: The subject of this sentence is erroneously linked to the adverbial clause.

Remedy: "**The reason** for his absence yesterday **is that** he was sick." or "John was sick yesterday."

Prescription: Avoid writing "The reason . . . is because." Use "The reason is / was that. . . ." "The reason the plan lost by such a wide margin was that landowners failed to get a consensus." Or use the "because" clause without "the reason is." "The plan lost by such a wide margin because the landowners failed to get a consensus."

RESPECTFULLY / RESPECTIVELY (adverb)

Symptom: "The goddess Artemis was not interested in cultivating the land or harnessing the forces of nature; she left those responsibilities to Demeter and Athena, **respectfully**."

Diagnosis: The adverb "respectfully" is used in error here.

Remedy: "The goddess Artemis was not interested in cultivating the land or harnessing the forces of nature; she left those responsibilities to Demeter and Athena, **respectively**."

Prescription: The meaning of "respectfully" is "courteously" or "feeling or manifesting veneration." "The Japanese businessman bowed respectfully to his associates." The meaning of "respectively" is "in the order given." "He credited his father and his mother for his good looks and intelligence, respectively." If you are unsure of a word's meaning, look it up in the dictionary.

RUN HIM OVER (verb, object pronoun, preposition)

Symptom: "A second driver tried to **run him over** after the first rear-ended his car."
Diagnosis: In this sentence, "over" is misplaced.
Remedy: "A second driver tried to **run over him** after the first rear-ended his car."
Prescription: One may "carry," "walk," "send," or "run" something "over" to a person or a location. "The courier ran the package over to the dealer." Or one may "run" something "over" something else. "He ran his fingers over the peach." Or one may "run over" someone or something with a vehicle. "The woman aimed her Mercedes-Benz at her husband and ran over him as he pleaded for her to stop."

SAFE HAVEN (adjective, noun)

Symptom: "Baghdad is no longer a **safe haven** for terrorists."

Diagnosis: "Safe" is redundant here.

Remedy: "Baghdad is no longer a **haven** for terrorists."

Prescription: The noun "haven" already means "a safe place." Avoid duplication. "A free Iraq will deny Al Quaeda terrorists a haven."

---

sequence of tenses

Symptom: "**Since he has announced** his intention to run for a city council seat, many people **contacted** him."

Diagnosis: The past tense forms are confused.

Remedy: "**Since he announced** his intention to run for a city council seat, many people **have contacted** him." or "**After he announced** his intention of running for a city council seat, many people **contacted** him."

Prescription: Use the simple past tense in a subordinate clause introduced by "since," "although," or "because" when the main verb is in the past tense. "Because the roof fell in, Charles has been living in a tent in the back yard." or "Because the roof fell in, Charles set up a tent in the back yard." "Since my baby left me, I found a new place to dwell." "Although Elvis left the building many years ago, his fans have continued to revere him."

SERVICE / SERVE (verb)

Symptom: "The owner of the shop **has serviced** thousands of customers over the years." or "employees who **service** this community."

Diagnosis: The meanings of "serve" and "service" are confused here.

Remedy: "The owner of the shop **has served** thousands of customers over the years." or "employees who **serve** this community."

Prescription: Use "serve" with people or things. "The waiter served his customers." "She serves tea to her guests every afternoon." Use "service" with things or animals. "The mechanic serviced the car." "The prized stallion services many mares."

SOMEONE (pronoun)

Symptom: "If **someone** you know is treating you poorly, ask **them** if there is something in **their lives** that may be causing **them** to feel bad about **themselves**."

Diagnosis: Here, the plural forms "them," "their," and "themselves" refer to the singular "someone."

Remedy: "If **someone** you know is treating you poorly, ask

him if there is something in **his life** that may be causing **him** to feel bad about **himself**." or "If someone you know is treating you poorly, ask **her** if there is something in **her life** that may be causing **her** to feel bad about **herself**."

Prescription: When referring to "someone," use singular pronouns "him" and "her," and singular possessive adjectives "his" and "her," "The detective noted that someone had left her purse behind."

SORT OF A (noun, preposition, indefinite article)

Symptom: "The official plans to impose some **sort of a** cap on spending."

Diagnosis: In this sentence, "a" is unnecessary.

Remedy: "The official plans to impose some **sort of** cap on spending." or "The official plans to impose **a** cap on spending."

Prescription: Avoid using an article after "sort of." "What sort of man would torture a child?"

---

split infinitive

Symptom: "The board decided **to not appeal** a court ruling."

Diagnosis: "Not" is used in error between "to" and its verb.

Remedy: "The board decided **not to appeal** a court ruling."

Prescription: Put "not," "always," "never," and other modifiers in front of infinitives. "Sylvia begged her mother not to send her to her room to watch television." "Grant tried always to be on time." "The teacher warned the students never to split an infinitive."

SPOT ON (adjective phrase)

Symptom: "The legislative analyst was **spot on** when she estimated that economic performance in 2008 might be weaker than budget officials had predicted."

Diagnosis: This sentence contains a British slang phrase.

Remedy: "The legislative analyst was **correct** when she estimated that economic performance in 2009 might be weaker than budget officials had predicted."

Prescription: Avoid using slang in formal writing.

-SQUARE-FEET (adjective, noun)

Symptom: "Plans have been approved for a 115,000-square-**feet** library and media center."
Diagnosis: The plural form "feet" is used erroneously in this sentence.
Remedy: "Plans have been approved for a 115,000-square-**foot** library and media center."
Prescription: If a quantifying word or phrase is followed by a noun or a noun phrase, use the singular form of the quantity. "The community built a four-million-dollar hospital." "Tex always wore a ten-gallon hat, even indoors." "Herbert's father owned fifty head of cattle." "Bets were placed in ten-cent increments." "Lawrence felt as if he had been hit by a ten-ton truck."

STEPPED FOOT (adjective, noun)

Symptom: "Finally they **stepped foot** on the soil of the coast."
Diagnosis: The intransitive verb "stepped" is used in error with a direct object. The word "foot" is redundant here.
Remedy: "Finally they **set foot** on the soil of the coast." or "Finally they **stepped** on the soil of the coast."
Prescription: "Step" already means "put down or press the foot." Use either "step" or "set foot." "Mr. X bought the building without ever setting foot in it." "After the cow stepped on his foot, Morey went to the hospital."

subject-verb agreement

Symptom: "From this **has sprung** active state **organizations**."
Diagnosis: The subject of this sentence is "organizations," a plural noun. The verb "has sprung" is singular.
Remedy: "From this **have sprung** active state **organizations**."
Prescription: Use a singular verb with a singular subject and a plural verb with a plural subject. "On what topics does the gentleman wish to speak?" "From what source have these secrets leaked?"

subject-verb agreement

Symptom: "The plight of homeless people **are** the legitimate concern of several agencies."
Diagnosis: The plural verb "are" does not agree with the singular subject "plight."
Remedy: "The plight of homeless people **is** the legitimate concern of several agencies."
Prescription: Use a singular verb with a singular subject. "The price of gas and oil has risen."

subject-verb agreement

Symptom: "The inmate and one of three guards **was** injured."

Diagnosis: Two people were injured, but the verb is singular here.

Remedy: "The inmate and one of three guards **were** injured."

Prescription: Use a plural verb with a plural subject. "His two sisters and his older brother have founded a promising new business."

subject-verb agreement

Symptom: "What will happen unless more money and attention **is paid** to increasing the number of new nurses?"

Diagnosis: The singular verb "is paid" does not agree with the compound subject "money and attention."

Remedy: "What will happen unless more money and attention **are paid** to increasing the number of new nurses?"

Prescription: Use a plural verb with a plural subject. "Tofu and wheat grass are becoming more popular."

THAN ANY (preposition, adjective)

Symptom: "California produces more food **than any** state in the nation."

Diagnosis: California is a state, too. Does it produce more food than itself?

Remedy: "California produces **more** food **than any other** state in the nation."

Prescription: Here, "any" means "one, no matter which, of more than two." Use "any other" after an unequal comparison. "Bill Gates has more money than any other American." "Mrs. X is less responsible than any other candidate."

THANKFULLY (adverb)

Symptom: "**Thankfully**, the pain has not returned."

Diagnosis: Here, "thankfully" is used erroneously as an independent adverb.

Remedy: "**She is thankful that** the pain has not returned." or "**Fortunately**, the pain has not returned."

Prescription: Avoid using "thankfully" as an independent

adverb. "All the orphans smiled thankfully at the nuns who had led them to safety." Do use "fortunately," "unfortunately," and "regrettably" independently to denote "It is fortunate," "It is unfortunate," and "It is regrettable."

THEIRSELVES (reflexive pronoun)

Symptom: "The group acknowledged that there was something greater than **theirselves**."
Diagnosis: The form "theirselves" is nonstandard or nonexistent.
Remedy: "The group acknowledged that there was something greater than **themselves**." or "The group acknowledged that there was something greater than **they**."
Prescription: Avoid using "theirselves" in formal writing. Use "themselves" instead. "The children were proud of themselves because they spelled all the words correctly."

THEM (plural object pronoun)

Symptom: "The days of calling up a commissioner and telling **them** what to do are over."
Diagnosis: In this sentence, the plural pronoun "them" refers to the singular noun "commissioner."

Remedy: "The days of calling up a commissioner and telling **him** what to do are over." or "The days of calling up a commissioner and telling **her** what to do are over."

Prescription: Make a pronoun agree in number with the noun it stands for. "If your cousin is rich, be nice to him." "The manager called each employee into his office and gave her a raise."

THEM HAVING (object pronoun, present participle)

Symptom: "Being connected to their faith is important to **them having** a productive life."

Diagnosis: The object of the preposition "to" is "having a productive life," not "them" in this sentence.

Remedy: "Being connected to their faith is important to **their having** a productive life." or "Being connected to one's faith is important to having a productive life."

Prescription: Avoid using a noun or a pronoun before a verbal phrase that serves as a noun. Use a possessive adjective, or rewrite the sentence more simply. "His having a one-hundredth birthday was a good reason to have a party." "No one objected to our putting on swimsuits and going for a swim."

THERE / THEIR (adverb / possessive adjective)

Symptom: "Dozens of families lost **there** homes in the hurricane."

Diagnosis: "There" is used in error here.

Remedy: "Dozens of families lost **their** homes in the hurricane."

Prescription: Use the adverb "there" to indicate "in that place." Use the possessive adjective "their" to indicate "belonging to them." "Their bones lie there now."

misplaced modifier

Symptom: "While **talking** to a friend on the phone**, my little dog** kept barking."

Diagnosis: "My little dog" is the subject of this sentence, and is talking and barking at the same time.

Remedy: "While **I was talking** to a friend on the phone**,** my little dog kept barking."

Prescription: Place a modifying phrase next to the person or thing it describes. "While Aunt Jess was making gravy, her sister set the table."

THEY (subject pronoun)

Symptom: "When involved with the care of a spouse, one can easily lose sight of what could happen if **they, the caregiver**, should fall ill along the way."

Diagnosis: In this sentence, "caregiver" is singular. The pronoun "they," which refers to "caregiver," is plural.

Remedy: "When involved with the care of a spouse, one can easily lose sight of what could happen if **she, the caregiver,** should fall ill along the way." or "When involved with the care of a spouse, one can easily lose sight of what could happen if **he, the caregiver,** should fall ill along the way." or "When involved with the care of a spouse, one can easily lose sight of what could happen if **the caregiver** should fall ill along the way."

Prescription: Make a pronoun agree in number with the noun it replaces. "The kindergarten teacher gave stars to all her pupils that day because they had all recited the alphabet perfectly."

THIS KIND OF A (adjective, noun, preposition, indefinite article)

Symptom: "Hardly any agencies reveal **this kind of a** mistake."
Diagnosis: Here, "a" is unnecessary.
Remedy: "Hardly any agencies reveal **this kind** of mistake."
Prescription: Avoid using an article after "this kind of." "This kind of rose is quite common." "Mona has always adored this kind of summer day."

THIS LARGE OF (adverb, adjective, preposition)

Symptom: "The company does not have enough cameras to monitor **this large of an area** adequately."
Diagnosis: "Large" is an adjective describing "area." "Of" is superfluous here.
Remedy: "The company does not have enough cameras to monitor **this large an area** adequately."
Prescription: Avoid using "of" with an adjective. "Not many people could eat this large a hamburger in one sitting."

TOO SMALL OF (adverb, adjective, preposition)

Symptom: "The world is **too small of a place** to carry out such unilateral policies."
Diagnosis: The world is "a place," not an "of a place." "Of" is unnecessary here.
Remedy: "The world is **too small a place** to carry out such unilateral policies."
Prescription: Avoid using "of" with an adjective. "Moving the grand piano was too difficult a task for one man." Or leave out the synonym phrase. "Moving the grand piano was too difficult for one man."

TRY AND / TRY TO (verb, conjunction / verb, infinitive)

Symptom: "They were pleased to see the group come together again to **try and move** forward."
Diagnosis: In this sentence, the group seems to have to do two things: "try" and "move."
Remedy: "They were pleased to see the group come together again to **try to** move forward."
Prescription: Use "try to," "need to,", ought to."

TURN INTO / TURN IN TO (verb, preposition / verb, adverb, preposition)

Symptom: "They charged the man with killing the girl to keep her from turning him **into** authorities for illegal activities."

Diagnosis: In this sentence, the man becomes the authorities, as if the girl had magic powers.

Remedy: "They charged the man with killing the girl to keep her from turning him **in to** authorities for illegal activities."

Prescription: "Turn into" means "change to the form of." "Turn in to" means "hand over to" or "report (someone) to." Distinguish between turning someone or something "into" someone or something else and turning someone "in to" an authority. "The magician turned his cane into a bouquet." "The illegal immigrants were turned in to the ICE."

UNBEKNOWNST (adjective)

Symptom: "**Unbeknownst** to his father, Jerry had been shoplifting."

Diagnosis: The word "unbeknownst" is a tedious variant of the obsolete "unbeknown."
Remedy: "**Without his father's knowledge**, Jerry had been shoplifting."
Prescription: Avoid using "unbeknownst" in formal writing in the United States.

UNHEALTHY / UNHEALTHFUL (adjective)

Symptom: "Some chefs fear that the squids' ink may be **unhealthy**."
Diagnosis: The ink is in poor physical condition here. Shall we call a doctor?
Remedy: "Some chefs fear that the squids' ink may be **unhealthful**."
Prescription: "Unhealthy" means "sick." "Unhealthful" means "not promoting well-being." Distinguish between "unhealthy" and "unhealthful" for your own well-being.

---

unparallel construction

Symptom: "This product should not be used by women who are **pregnant, nursing, or may become pregnant**."
Diagnosis: "Pregnant" and "nursing" are adjectives; "may

become pregnant" is a verb phrase.

Remedy: "This product should not be used by women who **are** pregnant, **are** nursing, **or may become** pregnant."

Prescription: Use parallel constructions in a list. "People who love horses, riding, and ranch life seldom live in a big city."

---

unparallel construction

Symptom: "Mr. X guided the college through **record enrollment**; **a major rebuilding effort** after the earthquake; and **oversaw the construction** of new performing arts, science, and computer centers."

Diagnosis: This sentence lacks parallelism. "Oversaw the construction" is not like "record enrollment" and "a major rebuilding effort."

Remedy: "Mr. X guided the college through **record enrollment**; **a major rebuilding effort** after the earthquake; and **the construction** of new performing arts, science, and computer centers."

Prescription: Make sure that items in a list are the same part of speech. "The president-elect is a man of good character, strong ethics, and sound judgment."

---

unparallel construction

Symptom: "Goals give us **purpose, direction,** and **help** us maintain our personal stability."

Diagnosis: "Purpose" and "direction" are nouns. "Help" is a verb.

Remedy: "Goals give us **purpose and direction,** and **help** us maintain our personal stability."

Prescription: Make sure that items in a list are the same part of speech. "We usually ordered popcorn, a soda, and candy when we went to the movies."

unparallel construction

Symptom: "Contestants choose **to** either **compete** as a team or **as individuals**."

Diagnosis: This sentence lacks parallelism. "To compete" is not like "as individuals."

Remedy: "Contestants choose to compete either **as a team** or **as individuals**."

Prescription: Use words that are the same part of speech after "either" and "or." "The applicants are either too young or too old." "You may either go or stay." "Either the mayor or the councilwoman will attend the ribbon-cutting ceremony." "Either she was mistaken, or she really did see a ghost."

unparallel construction

Symptom: "The search is on to identify all **its health risks, its sources**, and **to make** polluters pay for cleaning it up."

Diagnosis: This sentence lacks parallelism. "To make" is not like "its health risks" and "its sources."

Remedy: "The search is on to identify all **its health risks, its sources**, and **its cleanup costs**." or "The search is on **to identify** all its health risks **and** its sources, and **to make** polluters pay for cleaning it up."

Prescription: Make sure that items in a list are the same part of speech. Rewrite the sentence if you have to. "Joe wanted the woman's name, address, and telephone number."

unparallel construction

Symptom: "The officials would not allow the report to be circulated **either inside the CIA** or **the community**."

Diagnosis: This sentence lacks parallelism. "Inside the CIA" is not like "the community."

Remedy: "The officials would not allow the report to be circulated inside **either the CIA** or **the community**." or "The officials would not allow the report to be circulated either **inside the CIA** or **within the community**."

Prescription: Use constructions that are the same part of speech after "either" and "or." "The landlord told the renter either to pay up or to get out."

_____

_____

_____

_____

unparallel construction

Symptom: "Laser therapy helps **to reduce cravings, stress,** and **restores** balance to the body."

Diagnosis: This sentence needs parallel constructions. "To reduce cravings" is an infinitive phrase, "stress" is a noun, and "restores" is a verb.

Remedy: "Laser therapy helps to **reduce** cravings, **alleviate** stress, and **restore** balance to the body." or "Laser therapy **helps** to reduce cravings and stress, and it **restores** balance to the body."

Prescription: Use constructions that are the same part of speech in a list. Rewrite the sentence if you have to. "The regulations were established in order to reduce the amount of trash on the ground, to improve the beauty of the park, and to allow families to enjoy picnics there."

_____

_____

_____

_____

URBAN (adjective)

Symptom: "The initiative calls for extending the **city's urban** boundary."
Diagnosis: "Urban" is an adjective meaning "of the city." It is redundant here.
Remedy: "The initiative calls for extending the **city's** boundary." or "The initiative calls for extending the **urban** boundary."
Prescription: Avoid needless words.

UTILIZE (verb)

Symptom: "To protect your private information, we **utilize** Secure Socket Layer encryption."
Diagnosis: Here, a big word has been used unnecessarily.
Remedy: "To protect your private information, we **use** Secure Socket Layer encryption."
Prescription: "Utilize" means "turn to practical use." "We utilized the bucket as a makeshift seat." Avoid using a big word where a diminutive, monosyllabic one will suffice.

VERY UNIQUE (adjective)

Symptom: "The ancient Chinese vase had a **very unique** color."
Diagnosis: Here, "very" is unnecessary.
Remedy: "The ancient Chinese vase had a **unique** color."
Prescription: "Unique" means "sole, unequaled." Avoid using qualifying modifiers with "unique." "Now it is the public's turn to experience this unique addition to the landscape at today's grand-opening ceremony."

WAIT ON / WAIT FOR (verb with preposition)

Symptom: "He has done what he could and must now **wait on** the results."
Diagnosis: In this sentence, "wait on" is used in error with things rather than with people.
Remedy: "He has done what he could and must now **wait for** the results."
Prescription: One waits for a train, one's sweetheart, a holiday, an opportunity. One waits on customers, diners, and other people one serves.

WE, THE PEOPLE (pronoun, noun phrase)

Symptom: The plaque is dedicated to **we**, the people.
Diagnosis: Here, the nominative form of a pronoun is used in error after a preposition.
Remedy: The plaque is dedicated to **us**, the people.
Prescription: Use the object pronoun "us" after a preposition: "to us," "for us," with us," "about us."

WE / US (subject pronoun / object pronoun)

Symptom: "The action of the administration is a disservice to **we** Americans."
Diagnosis: The subject pronoun "we" is used in error after the preposition "to."
Remedy: "The action of the administration is a disservice to **us** Americans."
Prescription: After a preposition, use the objective form of pronouns: "to us," for them," "with her," "instead of him." "The plaque was dedicated to us, the firemen who had saved many lives."

WELL-INTENTIONED (adjective)

Symptom: "All too often, state and federal courts have found previous **well-intentioned** proposals invalid."

Diagnosis: Even though the writer may have good intentions, this sentence can be improved.

Remedy: "All too often, state and federal courts have found previous **well-intended** proposals invalid."

Prescription: Use "intention" as a noun. Use "intended" as an adjective. "Leroy had good intentions, but bad behavior." "His well-intended remarks insulted the senators nevertheless."

WELL WISHES (adverb, noun)

Symptom: "The parents sent their **well wishes** to the PTA president."

Diagnosis: An adverb is used in error to modify a noun here.

Remedy: "The parents sent their **good wishes** to the PTA president."

Prescription: Avoid using an adverb to modify a noun. Use an adjective instead. "Giselle wished the soldier well, and sent letters of good wishes to his buddies, too."

WHILST (conjunction)

Symptom: "Sylvia busied herself with cleaning chores **whilst** her husband watched the football game on television."

Diagnosis: The word "whilst" is seriously out of date.

Remedy: "Sylvia busied herself with cleaning chores **while** her husband watched the football game on television."

Prescription: Avoid using the word "whilst" in formal writing in the United States. Use "while" or "as" instead. "Nero fiddled while Rome burned." "Manuel whistled as he worked."

WHITHER / WITHER (adverb / verb)

Symptom: "The daylight shortens, the temperature dips, and the plants **whither**."

Diagnosis: The adverb "whither" is used in error as a verb here.

Remedy: "The daylight shortens, the temperature dips, and the plants **wither**."

Prescription: "Whither" means "to where?" Leave "whither" to Shakespeare. It is outmoded. "Wither" means "dry up, wilt, shrivel." "After only three days, the roses withered and drooped." If you are unsure how to spell a word, look it up in the dictionary.

WHO (subject pronoun)

*Symptom***:** "The youth, **who** authorities did not identify, escaped from custody."

Diagnosis: In this sentence, the subject form of the pronoun "who" is used as the direct object of a verb.

Remedy: "The youth, **whom** authorities did not identify, escaped from custody."

Prescription: Use "whom" as the direct object of a verb or as the object of a preposition "The old woman, whom he had known for many years, did not recognize him." "Send not to know for whom the bell tolls." Test by substituting "him," "her", or "them" for "whom." "Authorities did not identify him." "State law defines them as 'elders.'" Omit "whom" when it is redundant. "Is that the girl whom you know?" can be changed to "Is that the girl you know?"

WHOEVER YOU LIKE (subject pronoun, subject pronoun, verb)

Symptom: "Take **whoever** you like to the dance."

Diagnosis: In this sentence, the subject pronoun "whoever" is used as the direct object of "like."

Remedy: "Take **whomever** you like to the dance."

Prescription: Use the objective form of a pronoun when it is a direct object. "Robert wants to thank whomever the bank manager sends to return his money." Test by substituting "him," her," or "them" for "whom." "Take her to the dance." "Robert wants to thank him."

WHOM (object pronoun)

Symptom: "**Whom** does your family figure **is** the victim?"

Diagnosis: The objective form "whom" is used as the subject of "is" here.

Remedy: "**Who** does your family figure **is** the victim?"

Prescription: Use "who" as the subject of a verb. "Fred called his daughter, who he thought would be with her boyfriend." "Who (shall I say) is calling?" "Who (do you think) is right?" Test by substituting "he," "she," or "they" for "who." "Does your family figure she is the victim?" "He thought she would be with her boyfriend."

TO WHOMEVER IS (preposition, object pronoun, verb)

Symptom: "These people would be more likely to represent the opposition to **whomever** is in power."
Diagnosis: Here, the objective form "whomever" is used in error as the subject of the verb "is."
Remedy: "These people would be more likely to represent the opposition to **whoever** is in power."
Prescription: When a preposition is followed by a clause, the clause has its own subject and verb, and does not depend on the preposition. "It is difficult to find a term of adequate condemnation for whoever started last week's wildfire." "Give the old bicycle to whoever wants it."

WITHOUT THEM GETTING   (preposition, object pronoun, participle)

Symptom: "If only you could say it **without them getting angry!**"
Diagnosis: In this sentence, the verbal noun phrase "getting angry," not "them," is the object of the preposition "without."
Remedy: "If only you could say it **without their getting angry!**"
Prescription: Use a possessive form before a verbal noun used as the object of a preposition. "The police never would have found the pistol without his leading them to the scene of the crime."

WITH SHE AND HER CHILDREN (prepositional phrase)

Symptom: "Mr. O'Malley was seen boarding the ship **with she and her children**."

Diagnosis: Here, the subject form "she" is used as the object of the preposition "with."

Remedy: "Mr. O'Malley was seen boarding the ship **with her and her children**."

Prescription: Avoid using a subject pronoun after a preposition. Use the objective form. Object pronouns are "me," "you," "him," "her," "it," "us," and "them." "Marco traveled to Italy with her and her mother."

WITHOUT THEM HAVING (prepositional phrase)

Symptom: "This would have taken effect **without them having** to take responsibility for it."

Diagnosis: The object of the preposition "without" is not "them," but rather "having."

Remedy: "This would have taken effect **without their having** to take responsibility for it."

Prescription: Use a possessive form between a preposition

and its object. "The covert investigation might have gone on without the CIA's having any knowledge of its existence."

WORST OF ANY   (superlative adjective, preposition, adjective)

Symptom: "Our state's highway and bridge conditions are among the **worst of any** state's."
Diagnosis: In this sentence, the superlative "worst" is used erroneously with "any."
Remedy: "Our state's highway and bridge conditions are among **the worst of all**." or "Our state's highway and bridge conditions are among **the worst** in the country."
Prescription: Use a superlative when comparing more than two things or people. Instead of "of any," write "of all." "We live in the best of all possible worlds."

WOULD HAVE TO HAVE BEEN   (conditional verb, perfect passive infinitive)

Symptom: "For the plan to have worked, all those participating **would have to have been** very broadminded."

Diagnosis: The tenses in the main clause are confused.

Remedy: "For the plan to have worked, all those participating **would have had to be** very broad-minded."

Prescription: Instead of writing a perfect infinitive after "would have," write "would have had," "would have liked," "world have hated," or the like. Then write the infinitive of the following verb. "Henry would have had to be crazy to take such a risk." "The eight-year-old would have liked to visit Disneyland every month if her mother had allowed her to go."

YOU / YOUR (pronoun, possessive adjective)

Symptom: "Please remit the co-payment for **you** and **your** child's office visits."

Diagnosis: The insurance payment is for the office visits, not fou you.

Remedy: "Please remit the co-payment for **your** and **your** child's office visits."

Prescription: Use a possessive form before the object of a preposition. "The coals glowed like the wizard's and his daughter's eyes." "The fourteen-year-old neighbor drove the car without my or my husband's permission."

ADDENDA: SOME USEFUL ITEMS

SOME GREEK AND LATIN PLURALS

ADDENDA (singular ADDENDUM, "something to be added, especially as a supplement to a book")
BACTERIA (singular BACTERIUM, "a microorganism that causes disease")
CANDELABRA (singular CANDELABRUM, "a large branched candlestick")
DATA (singular DATUM, "a thing given")
ERRATA (singular ERRATUM, "an error in a work already printed")
PHENOMENA (singular PHENOMENON, "any extremely unusual or extraordinary thing or occurrence")

DISTINCTIVE SUBJECT PRONOUNS

I, HE, SHE, THEY, WHO, WHOEVER

DISTINCTIVE OBJECT PRONOUNS

ME, HIM, HER, US, THEM, WHOM, WHOMEVER

"I BEFORE E, EXCEPT AFTER C, AND WHEN SOUNDED LIKE AY, AS IN NEIGHBOR AND WEIGH."

Exceptions to this rule include:

FANCIES and other plurals of words ending in *–cy*

FINANCIER
ATHEISM
ATHEIST
BEING
CAFFEINE
DEIFY
DEISM
DEITY
EITHER
FOREIGN
FEISTY
GEIGER
HEIGHT
HEIR
HEIST
HEREIN
NEITHER
SEISMIC
SEIZE
SEIZURE
SHEIK
SHEILA
THEIR
THEISM
THEIST
THEREIN
WEIR
WEIRD

GLOSSARY

(Definitions are from *Webster's New World College Dictionary, Fourth Edition*; examples are mine.)

Abbreviation: a shortened form of a word or phrase, e.g., *ASAP, no.2*.

Active: denoting the voice or form of a verb whose subject is the performer, or agent, of the action of the verb e.g., This dog *bites*.

Adjective: any of a class of words used to modify a noun or other substantive, as by describing qualities of the entity denoted, stating its limits or quantity, or distinguishing it from others, e.g., *heavy, huge, blue-green*.

Adverb: any of a class of words used generally to modify a verb, an adjective, another adverb, or a clause, by expressing time, place, manner, degree, cause, etc. English adverbs often end in *ly*, e.g., *slowly*.

Adverbial clause: a word group containing a subject and a verb that occurs in grammatical functions typical of adverbs, e.g., *whenever there was a full moon*.

Adverbial phrase: a word group that occurs in grammatical functions typical of adverbs, e.g, *every morning*.

Capital: the form of an alphabetical letter used to begin a sentence or proper name, e.g., *One Tuesday evening Pauline disappeared.*

Clause: a group of words containing a subject and a finite verb, usually forming part of a compound or complex sentence, e.g., *As soon as the bell had rung. . . .*

Comparative: designating or of the second degree of comparison of adjectives and adverbs; expressing a greater degree of a quality or attribute than that expressed in the positive degree, e.g., *bigger* or *more beautiful.*

Conditional: designating a word, clause, mood, or tense expressing a condition, as one beginning with *if*, e.g., *if I were you, if that is true.*

Conjunction: an uninflected word used to connect words, phrases, clauses, or sentences, e.g., *and, because.*

Conjunctive phrase: a group of words beginning with a conjunction, e.g., *as far as.*

Correlative: expressing mutual relation and used in pairs, e.g., *either . . . or.*

Definite article: *the.* The definite article refers to a specific person, thing, etc.

Direct object: the word or words denoting the thing or person that receives the action of a transitive verb, e.g., Her kitten always used *the litter box.*

Disjunctive: indicating a contrast or an alternative between words, clauses, etc. e.g., *or.*

Gerund: a verbal noun ending in *ing*, e.g., They enjoy *skiing* in the Alps.

Idiom: a phrase, construction, or expression that differs from the usual or literal meaning, e.g., *He heard it on the grapevine.*

Indefinite article: *a, an.* The indefinite article does not refer to a specific person, thing, etc.

Infinitive: the form of the verb that expresses existence or action without reference to person, number, or tense and can also function as a noun. The infinitive is preceded by the word *to.*

Interjection: an exclamation inserted into an utterance without grammatical connection, e.g., *Aha!*

Intransitive: designating a verb that does not require a direct object, e.g., *come.*

Linking verb: a verb that functions chiefly as a connection between a subject and a predicate complement, e.g., *is, seem.*

Modifier: a word, phrase, or clause that limits the meaning of another word or phrase, e.g., *big, slowly, while she was sleeping.*

Noun: any of a class of words naming or denoting a person, place, thing, action, quality, etc., e.g., *man, Helena, eagerness.*

Object of a preposition: a noun or pronoun that is governed by a preposition, e.g. for *years*, with *him.*

Object pronoun: a pronoun form used as the object of a verb or of a preposition, e.g., *me, you, him, her, it, us, them, this, those.*

Participle: a verbal form having some characteristics and functions of both verb and adjective, e.g., *smiling, closed.*

Passive: denoting the voice or form of a verb whose subject is the recipient of the action of the verb, e.g., *was bitten*.

Past: indicating an action completed or in progress at a former time, or a state or condition in existence at a former time, e.g., *went, were*.

Past participle: a participle used with auxiliaries to express, typically, completed action or a time or state gone by, e.g., has *finished*, is *gone*.

Past perfect: a tense indicating an action as completed before a specified or implied time in the past, e.g., *had left*.

Perfect: expressing or showing a state or action completed at the time of speaking or at the time indicated, e.g., *has left*.

Phrase: a sequence of two or more words conveying a single thought or forming a distinct part of a sentence but not containing a subject and a predicate, e.g., *while brushing her teeth*.

Plural: designating or of the category of number that refers to more than one person or thing, e.g., *eggs*.

Possessive adjective: designating or of a case, form, or construction expressing possession or some like relationship, e.g., *man's, ladies', his, her, its, our, your, their*.

Possessive pronoun: *mine, yours, his, hers, ours, theirs*.

Preposition: a relation or function word that connects a lexical word or a syntactical construction to another element of the sentence, e.g., *from* the country, *for* them, *of* his own.

Present participle: a participle used with auxiliaries to express present or continuing action or state of being, e.g., is *working*, were *going*, had been *grieving*.

Present perfect: a tense indicating an action as completed or a state as having ended at the time of speaking but not at any definite time in the past, e.g., *have eaten, is finished*.

Present: indicating action as now taking place, or state as now existing, or action that is habitual or always the same, e.g., *goes, are, takes, believe*.

Pronoun: any of a small class of relationship or signal words that assume the functions of nouns within clauses or phrases while referring to other locutions within the sentence or in other sentences, e.g., *I, me, who, whom, which, that, anyone, everyone*.

Quantifying: expressing the number or amount, e.g., *many, a few*.

Reflexive: designating or expressing a grammatical relation in which a verb's subject and an object in the sentence refer to the same person or thing, serving to indicate that the action of the verb is directed back to the subject, e.g., Harold cut a big piece of cake for *himself*. Maria killed *herself*.

Relative pronoun: a word that introduces a dependent clause and that refers to an antecedent, e.g., people *who* like chocolate, a problem *that* persists.

Sentence: a word or group of syntactically related words that states, asks, commands, or exclaims something, e.g., *"Get out!" Norma shouted at the intruder.*

Singular: designating or of the category of number that refers to only one person or thing, e.g., a *boy*, the *carpet*.

Subject: the noun or other substantive that is one of the two immediate constituents of a sentence and about which something is said in the predicate, e.g., *The hurricane destroyed thousands of buildings.*

Superlative: designating or of the extreme degree of comparison of adjectives and adverbs; expressing the greatest degree of the quality or attribute expressed by the positive degree, e.g., *wildest, most humbly.*

Subordinate clause: a clause that cannot function as a complete sentence by itself but has a nominal, adjectival, or adverbial function within a larger sentence.

Tense: a characteristic of verbs that indicates the time of the action or state of being that a verb expresses. Tenses in English are usually listed as *present, past, future, present perfect, past perfect (pluperfect)* and *future perfect.* Tenses other than the simple present (e.g., *like*) and the simple past (e.g., *liked*) are formed by the use of an auxiliary verb with a participle or an infinitive.

Transitive: expressing an action thought of as passing over to and having an effect on some person or thing; taking a direct object; said of certain verbs, e.g., The aroma *filled* the room.

Verb: any of a class of words expressing action, existence, or occurrence, or used as an auxiliary or copula, and usually constituting the main element of a predicate, e.g., *go, is, happened, should.*